A CHOICE OF
SCOTTISH VERSE
1470-1570

Selected with an introduction by
John and Winifred MacQueen

FABER AND FABER
3 Queen Square
London

First published in 1972
by Faber and Faber Limited
3 Queen Square London WC1
Printed in Great Britain by
Robert MacLehose and Company Limited
The University Press Glasgow

ISBN 0 571 09686 7
(Faber Paper Covered Edition)

ISBN 0 571 09532 1
(Hard Bound Edition)

A Choice of Scottish Verse
1470–1570

ACKNOWLEDGEMENTS

For permission to use some of the material in this volume, we are grateful to the Trustees of the National Library of Scotland and to the Council of the Scottish Text Society. We are also grateful to Mrs. Angela West who has typed a difficult manuscript with accuracy and forbearance.

CONTENTS

CONTENTS

INTRODUCTION

This anthology opens with a hymn to the Virgin and concludes with a song of triumph over the fallen Roman Catholic hierarchy. Many of the intermediate poems are satires, or at least commentaries, on aspects of the condition of Scotland, as contemporary poets saw it. This emphasis on involvement, as it has come to be called, is not accidental. In Scotland the century between 1470 and 1570 witnessed, not only a brilliant development of poetry, but also a series of major social, intellectual and spiritual changes culminating in the Reformation and the expulsion of Queen Mary. The poetry was affected by the changes in a way which the anthology will, I hope, help to make clear. Elsewhere the nearest parallel is with the literature of another period of revolutionary change, the late seventeenth and earlier eighteenth century in England. For Scottish poetry, the century is an Augustan era, when life and letters were related very much as later they came to be in the poetry of Dryden and Pope. The parallel extends to the value set on poetic craftsmanship. Stylistic decorum and finish mattered as much to Henryson, Dunbar and their fellows as to any English Augustan. The poets were *makaris*, craftsmen, using an instrument, the delicacy and precision of which has not often been acknowledged (or surpassed) by later generations.

The poetry belongs primarily to the court, if that term is extended to include the households of the greater nobility and churchmen. The court background of Dunbar, Douglas, Lindsay and Alexander Scott is explicit. Henryson's later connections were with the abbey of Dunfermline, which maintained a relationship to the Scottish crown almost as intimate as that of Westminster Abbey to the English. Court poetry in Scotland, however, remained in close touch with life outside court circles. Partly this resulted from the relative poverty of the country — the resources and interests of the moderately prosperous burgess were closer to those of the labourer and the lesser nobleman than was usual in other countries. Family loyalties too were tenacious and extensive and ranged across class divisions. The feudal system had never established itself as thoroughly in Scotland as England, and to a great extent it had collapsed during the wars of independence (1296–1328). Military necessity had established a strong sense of the community of Scotland as a whole. There is little to suggest, finally, that the Stewart monarchs saw any particular merit in class-divisions; their interest lay rather in the cultivation of good relationships with other classes against the nobility than in maintaining any rigid division between nobleman and commoner. Almost inevitably the poetry of the makaris combined the courtly with the popular.

Of all the poets represented, Dunbar, who in some ways is the most individual, contrives also to remain the closest to the European courtly norm. He is a considerable writer, not primarily because his verse transcends court values, but by virtue of the honesty (often self-centred and embittered) which forces him to realize the gap in those values between pretension and reality. This honesty, in turn, results from a vivid awareness, not in itself uncourtly, of the traditional Four Last Things — death, judgement, hell and heaven — an awareness to which he gives recurrent expression. It is the basis, for instance, of the lyrical and personal 'Meditatioun in Wyntir'. It is the standard by which the court is judged in 'None may Assure in this Warld':

> Quhat help is thair in lordschips sevin,
> quhone na hous is bot hell and hevin,
> palice of lycht, or pit obscure . . . ?

'Lament for the Makaris' is an extended Dance of Death. 'The Dance of the Sevin Deidly Synnis' plays comic but horrifying variations on the theme of death and judgement — and again there is an obvious, if generally only implied, relevance to court life. Sometimes it reaches the surface:

> allace! that courtis of noble kingis
> of thame can nevir be quyte.

The verbal energy of the hymns on the Nativity and Resurrection results from Dunbar's powerful awareness of the forces which Christ overcame, and which dominate the other poems.

Dunbar, one should remember, was priest as well as courtier. Like several of his fellow poets, he was also a university graduate. (Henryson probably graduated from a continental university: Dunbar, Douglas and Lindsay were graduates of the oldest Scottish university, St. Andrews, founded in 1411.) Their university education helps to explain the fact that the work of all four shows traces of the northern Renaissance. In terms of pure Latin scholarship, the greatest Scottish humanists were Hector Boece (c. 1465–c. 1536) and George Buchanan (1506–1582). One cannot however ignore the work of the vernacular poets.

Dunbar's relationship to the movement is palpably more tangential than that of Henryson or Douglas, but is quite perceptible. He lacks, for instance, the traditional modesty of the medieval poet about his own works, and on occasions shows an artistic confidence as self-assertive (and accurate) as anything in Horace, Benvenuto Cellini or Shakespeare. With Horace's almost over-familiar

> *Exegi monumentum aere perennius*
> *regalique situ pyramidum altius,*
> *quod non imber edax, non Aquilo impotens*
> *possit diruere aut innumerabilis*
> *annorum series et fuga temporum,*
> (*Odes* III. 30)

one should compare

> *als lang in mynd my wark sall hald,*
> *als haill in everie circumstance,*
> *in forme, in mater, and substance,*
> *but wering or consumptioun,*
> *roust, canker, or corruptioun,*
> *as ony of thair werkis all.*

INTRODUCTION

These lines separate the two catalogues of the king's servitors, the worthy and the worthless, which in bulk form the greater part of 'Remonstrance to the King', and which for most people seem to disguise the classical subtlety and merit of the poem. Dr. Tom Scott, for instance, perhaps the most generally sympathetic critic who has yet written on Dunbar, finds this to say in comment: 'Despite the tediousness of the catalogue device and the weakness of the flyting, the poem has dignity — not always a feature of Dunbar in his satiric-querulous mood — and structure: it has nobility, manliness, courage, and the outspoken assertion of the rights of real merit. These are no minor virtues in any poem by any poet.' So far as it goes, I agree with Dr. Scott's commendation, but I cannot agree with his condemnation of the catalogues and the flyting, and indeed I shall venture to suggest that because he has not done them justice, Dr. Scott has missed much of the point of the poem.

In the opening two paragraphs, the generally dignified metre and style partially conceals — and so, of course, renders more effective — the irony which increases from line to line. In the first four couplets, for instance, one notices the number of near-magicians among the apparently laudable court officers — 'divinouris', 'philosophouris' (= 'alchemists') and 'astrologis', professions which Dunbar generally held in contempt. Nor in a renaissance court were the professions of law and medicine necessarily admirable. The words 'courtmen' and 'kirkmen' too may have unsavoury overtones. The catalogue, in other words, is less simply laudatory than it seems, and this fact helps to prepare the reader for the otherwise extraordinary fact that the aristocratic Dunbar seems not only to regard with complacency the favour which James IV lavished on 'pryntouris, payntouris and potingaris', but also to regard his own station as properly inferior to that of such men:

> *And thocht that I, amang the laif,*
> *unworthy be ane place to have,*
> *or in thair nummer to be tald.*

It is here in particular that Dr. Scott misses the irony. Dunbar is unworthy, not because his art is inferior, but because to all men of right judgement its value wholly transcends that of the others, however little king and court may recognise the fact. The contrast of courtly obtuseness with permanent artistic value is the centre, not merely of the opening, but of the poem as a whole, and is all the stronger for the tension between implied and apparent meaning in the first seventeen couplets. The irony, in other words, gains much of its dynamic from the apparently feeble catalogue form.

The tension breaks in the denunciatory energy of the next nineteen couplets. In those the energy is at least partly derived from metrical modulations, with which Dunbar combines heavier alliteration and a good deal of internal rhyme and assonance. Compare, for instance, the mild alliteration and metrical inversion in the line already quoted:

> *pryntouris, payntouris, and potingaris,*

least partly because he possesses no extensive coherent
body of general principles and ideas from which his
poetry may grow. Henryson's virtuosity with language
and metre is less ostentatious than Dunbar's, and so
to some extent has passed unnoticed. His greatness is
most plainly to be seen in the range of general principles
and ideas which informs his poetry and allows it to
encompass tragedy and comedy alike. Henryson is more
Shakespearian than Dunbar.

Henryson's comedy and tragedy are both represented
in this collection — comedy by the linked series of beast
fables which George Bannatyne called *The Tod*; tragedy
by *The Testament of Cresseid*. Because the stylistic and
other differences between the two are self-evident, I intend
to limit the present discussion to the rather less obvious
similarities and parallelisms.

Although we know little about Henryson's career, the
fact that he was a canon and civil lawyer has been
established in terms partly of the records, partly of the
references to legal points and procedures which abound
in his works. In one sense, then, Henryson possessed a
legal mind. It was not, however, a mind limited to points
of law and procedure. Equity rather than statute law was
his major concern — a concern which merged in-
evitably into problems of natural and divine law, more
especially the relationship between apparent anarchy in
the world of human beings, the harsh inevitability of the
natural creation, and divine authority and mercy. It is
thus that *The Testament* and *The Tod* are linked.

The central episode of *The Testament* is the trial of

with the much more vigorous

> *soukaris, groukaris, gledaris, gunnaris.*

Partly too the effect of energy is a matter of vocabulary —
in the third paragraph at once more exotic and stylistically
lower than in the preceding two.

The reader also grows gradually aware that the two
groups of courtmen are not so clearly separable as the
formal structure of the poem might seem to suggest. The
artisans — shipwrights, masons, printers and so on — are
no longer relevant; their work lay outwith the court
itself; Dunbar's anger is directed against court habitués :

> *schulderaris, and schovaris, that hes no schame,*
> *and to no cunning that can clame;*
> *and can non uthir craft nor curis*
> *bot to mak thrang, Schir, in your duris.*

Those men, however, might very well be the same as the

> *divinouris, rethoris, and philosophouris,*
> *astrologis, artistis, and oratouris,*

seen from a different angle and through more jaundiced
eyes. The suspicion that this is so grows to a near certainty
when a reference to alchemists forms the climax of the
sorry list :

> *in quintiscence, eik, ingynouris joly,*
> *that far can multiplie in folie;*
> *fantastik fulis, bayth fals and gredy,*
> *off toung untrew, and hand evill deidie :*
> *few dar, of all this last additioun,*
> *cum in tolbuyth without remissioun.*

The reference is primarily to the doctor and alchemist, John Damian, abbot of Tungland in Kirkcudbright, and favourite of King James. It is at this point, I suggest, that it finally becomes clear that the first catalogue presents the court, not in reality, but from the point of view, let us say, of the deluded king. Reality, as seen by Dunbar alone, is to be found in the second catalogue. The king's philosophers are in fact 'ingynouris joly' and fantastik fulis'.

Dunbar reserves his best stroke for the last. Ostensibly, the poem is a begging address in a form which is as conventional as the dream vision, and almost as long established in courtly tradition — witness Chaucer's *Complaynt to his Purse* and Lydgate's *Letter to Gloucester*. In general, poems of this kind are humorous. Dunbar keeps to the convention, but his humour is more scathing than that of either earlier author. In his final paragraph he contrives a brilliant reversal of expectations:

> *And yit more panence wald I have,*
> *Had I rewarde amang the laif,*
> *it wald me sumthing satisfie,*
> *and les of my malancolie,*
> *and gar me mony falt ouerse,*
> *that now is brayd befoir myn e.*

Dunbar, in other words, endures melancholy as a consequence of lack of money, but his melancholy lets him see the truth, to which he might otherwise find himself persuaded to turn a blind eye. The final paragraph keeps to the begging convention, but at the same time confirms the truth of the previous denunciation, and establishes

that if Dunbar ever changes his tune, it wi[ll] because the court has improved, but becau[se] has been corrupted. The king's gifts are no[t] 'tryackill', a word which Professor Kinsle[y] 'medicine for venomous bites and maligna[nt] The malignant disease which afflicts D[unbar] ability to see the truth.

Not many poets exhibit a control of stru[cture] equal to that of Dunbar in 'Remonstranc[e] The nearest parallel which occurs to [me] dialogue between Ulysses and Tiresias ([on] the art of the *captator*, the fortune hunt[er] often described as the one in which H[orace] approaches the manner of Juvenal. I[t is by] Horace (the *Odes* as well as the *Satir[es]* that Dunbar's participation in the n[oble] must be judged.

In defiance of chronology, I have [placed] partly because he comes closest t[o the] tradition, partly because he is th[e greatest of] Scottish Renaissance poets. Indee[d] of Burns and McDiarmid, he is p[erhaps the greatest] of all Scottish poets. This pre-e[minence does] some injustice to other poets [and in] particular to the greatest of the[m] Dunbar's metrical and lingu[istic] effectiveness of his best poems, [together with] his emotional and intellectual [range, span] two great literary kinds, trag[edy and comedy,] depends on interplay of per[sonae]

B

INTRODUCTION

Cresseid before the planetary assembly. The charge, 'sclander and defame injurious', is laid by Cupid before the king, Phoebus, in his parliament, of which Mercury is 'foirspeikar'. The action is not contested. Saturn and Cynthia are made assessors to judge the penalty appropriate to the crime, and it is Cynthia who pronounces the 'sentence diffinityve'. The planets are the powers which govern the material creation, and their sentence, which is in strict accord with the laws of the material universe, transforms Cresseid's entire physical being, and apparently condemns her beyond redemption.

So far as it goes, the legal procedure is incontestable. At the same time, it misses everything which a court of celestial equity might reasonably consider as part of Cresseid's defence, and which Henryson takes good care to keep before the reader's attention. In Henryson, as in Chaucer, Cresseid is an attractive figure whose downfall has been caused as much by circumstance as by personal weakness. She is not the natural wanton of popular tradition:

> *Yit nevertheless quhat ever men deme or say*
> *in scornefull langage of thy brukkilnes,*
> *I sall excuse, als far furth as I may,*
> *thy womanheid, thy wisdome and fairnes:*
> *the quhilk Fortoun hes put to sic distres*
> *as hir pleisit, and nathing throw the gilt*
> *of thee, throw wickit langage to be spilt.*

Henryson comments only on the element of accident which plays so important a part in the establishment of

[19]

popular reputation or infamy. 'Nathing throw the gilt of thee' is the emotional exaggeration of a defence counsel, but it is exaggeration of a truth which the planetary court ignores.

The court also ignores the power over 'all thing generabill' held by its own members. Henryson's planets are the astrological forces which govern human activity so far as that does not result from divine intervention or the exercise of human free will. In particular, planetary action caused the rain which brought Troilus and Cresseid to the first consummation of their love, and planetary action afterwards forced Cresseid into Diomeid's power. The planets themselves, in other words, have caused the circumstances which led to Cresseid's downfall, and they also form the court which judges her consequent blasphemy — not the most equitable situation for a defendant. Such questions leave them unaffected:

> O cruell Saturne! fraward and angrie,
> hard is thy dome, and too malitious;
> on fair Cresseid quhy hes thou na mercie,
> quhilk was sa sweit, gentill and amorous?
> Withdraw thy sentence and be gracious
> as thou was never; so schawis thou thy deid,
> ane wraikfull sentence gevin on fair Cresseid.

In two ways only the situation remains outside planetary control. Cresseid possesses free will, which is capable of rising superior to astral determinism. The planets are not the ultimate authorities of the universe, but are the powerful instruments through which divine providence may fulfil itself, and which it may on occasion transcend. In the 'spittaill hous', Cresseid does not fall into despair, but by the exercise of free will teaches herself to accept the 'law of lipper leid'. Providence intervenes in Troilus' disinterested act of charity, which causes Cresseid to accept the responsibility for her own deeds, which she had previously refused to acknowledge. Henryson allows no relaxation of the physical punishment for her weakness, but the reader finds in her death after suffering the sense of justice and redemption which marks high tragedy. The action lends itself to Aristotelian analysis, moving us, as it does, to pity and terror — pity for Cresseid herself, terror at the powers she roused against herself — and by way of the peripeteia of Troilus's intervention, producing catharsis at the end.

The ostensible world of *The Testament* is pre-Christian, and divine justice in the context of paganism is the over-all theme. *The Tod* deals with divine and human justice in the declared context of medieval Christianity and at the lower level appropriate to comedy. In terms of plot, it is important to realise that each of the main characters suffers in precise accordance with his deserts. Measure for Measure is as important a theme for Henryson as for Shakespeare. Every major character in *The Tod* bears a precise responsibility for his own misfortunes — Chanteclere and the wolf pay the penalty for allowing themselves to be blinded by self-conceit and flattery; the elder fox failed to keep the terms of his penance; the younger broke the king's peace by killing a lamb. Admiration for the foxes' cleverness is counter-balanced by the helplessness of their victims — 'a littill kid' and the fattest of 'a trip of lambis dansand on a dike'. The stupidity as well as the cleverness of the foxes is emphasised — one stroking his belly as he basks in the sun, and saying

Upoun this bellye ware sett a bolt full mete;

the other forgetting himself a few moments after quoting the very apposite proverb, *felix quem faciunt aliena pericula cautum*. For the foxes in particular there is no possibility of urging mitigating circumstances. Their punishment exemplifies both divine and human justice.

In *The Testament* the retributory aspect of divine justice is symbolised by the planets, and at the same time it is linked to human justice by the concept of a high court, a parliament, of the planets. Henryson, in other words, separates ultimate divine mercy from planetary retributory justice, and more or less equates the latter with human justice. In *The Tod* the same elements combine somewhat differently. The planetary powers return in the second episode:

> *Than Saturne alde was enterit in Capricorne*
> *and Jupiter movit in Sigittarye*
> *and Mars up in the Rammys hede was borne*
> *and Phebus in the Lyoun furth coud carye,*
> *Venus the Crab, the Mone was in Aquarye,*
> *Mercurius, the god of eloquence,*
> *into the Virgin maid his residence.*

These however are not the terrifying deities of *The Testament*: Lourence sees merely

[22]

INTRODUCTION

the twinkling sternis clere
and all the planetis of the firmament.

They are powerful, but not merely retributory — Jupiter, for instance, in his house of Sagittarius is particularly favourable, as is Mercury in his exaltation in Virgo. These partly compensate for the adverse power of the Lord of the Ascendent, Saturn, the Greater Infortune, in his house of Capricorn. The planets, all this is to say, do not simply condemn Lourence as they did Cresseid; the universe is a Christian one, and the possibility of redemption remains evidently open in a way not possible for Cresseid. It is for this reason that the fox seeks a confessor. Had he been able to keep the very modest penance imposed by Friar Wolf Waitskath, he might have won his own salvation. His behaviour, however, left him open to the more malignant heavenly influences, and he was killed in the full enjoyment of his sin.

The universe of the poem is Christian; the animals who inhabit it are types of fallen man. Human justice, represented by the lion and his court, the parliament of four-footed beasts, is as fallible as the individual animals, a fact seen most clearly in the relationship of the court to the 'gray stude meir' who refuses to attend the assembly. Here, as usually in Henryson, it is essential to take the *Moralitas* into consideration:

> *This mere is men of contemplatioun,*
> *off pennance walkand in this wildernace,*
> *as monkis and othir men of religioun*
> *that presis God to pleis in every place,*

> *abstrackit fra this warldis wretchidnes,*
> *in wilful povertee fra pomp and pride,*
> *and fra this warld in mind ar mortifyde.*

Clearly the mare's refusal to attend is entirely proper and praiseworthy. It is equally clear, even to the fox, that the primary function of the court should be to suppress such wrongdoers as Fader wer himself:

> *I wait this suddane semblay that I se,*
> *havand the poyntis of a parliament,*
> *is maid to mar sic misdoaris as me.*

The court however makes Fader wer its emissary to force the gray mare, whom it considers contumacious, to compear. When eventually the fox does pay the extreme penalty, it is not for his life of crime, but for an act of lese-majesty, the stupidity of which he should himself have been the first to realise.

The Tod thus establishes an over-all satiric contrast between the fits and starts of human justice (indeed of human activity in general) and the equitable operation of providence as revealed through the stars. Henryson puts the contrast into a specifically Scottish context. The lion, the king of beasts, is the heraldic emblem of the King of Scotland, and when he says:

> *I lat you wit my mycht is merceabill*
> *and steris none that ar to me prostrat,*

he is quoting the Scottish regal motto, *parcere prostratis scit nobilis ira leonis*. (His name, Nobill, derives from the French beast-epic, but also refers to the same motto.) It

with the much more vigorous

> *soukaris, groukaris, gledaris, gunnaris.*

Partly too the effect of energy is a matter of vocabulary — in the third paragraph at once more exotic and stylistically lower than in the preceding two.

The reader also grows gradually aware that the two groups of courtmen are not so clearly separable as the formal structure of the poem might seem to suggest. The artisans — shipwrights, masons, printers and so on — are no longer relevant; their work lay outwith the court itself; Dunbar's anger is directed against court habitués:

> *schulderaris, and schovaris, that hes no schame,*
> *and to no cunning that can clame;*
> *and can non uthir craft nor curis*
> *bot to mak thrang, Schir, in your duris.*

Those men, however, might very well be the same as the

> *divinouris, rethoris, and philosophouris,*
> *astrologis, artistis, and oratouris,*

seen from a different angle and through more jaundiced eyes. The suspicion that this is so grows to a near certainty when a reference to alchemists forms the climax of the sorry list:

> *in quintiscence, eik, ingynouris joly,*
> *that far can multiplie in folie;*
> *fantastik fulis, bayth fals and gredy,*
> *off toung untrew, and hand evill deidie:*
> *few dar, of all this last additioun,*
> *cum in tolbuyth without remissioun.*

INTRODUCTION

The reference is primarily to the doctor and alchemist, John Damian, abbot of Tungland in Kirkcudbright, and favourite of King James. It is at this point, I suggest, that it finally becomes clear that the first catalogue presents the court, not in reality, but from the point of view, let us say, of the deluded king. Reality, as seen by Dunbar alone, is to be found in the second catalogue. The king's philosophers are in fact 'ingynouris joly' and fantastik fulis'.

Dunbar reserves his best stroke for the last. Ostensibly, the poem is a begging address in a form which is as conventional as the dream vision, and almost as long established in courtly tradition — witness Chaucer's *Complaynt to his Purse* and Lydgate's *Letter to Gloucester*. In general, poems of this kind are humorous. Dunbar keeps to the convention, but his humour is more scathing than that of either earlier author. In his final paragraph he contrives a brilliant reversal of expectations:

> *And yit more panence wald I have,*
> *Had I rewarde amang the laif,*
> *it wald me sumthing satisfie,*
> *and les of my malancolie,*
> *and gar me mony falt ouerse,*
> *that now is brayd befoir myn e.*

Dunbar, in other words, endures melancholy as a consequence of lack of money, but his melancholy lets him see the truth, to which he might otherwise find himself persuaded to turn a blind eye. The final paragraph keeps to the begging convention, but at the same time confirms the truth of the previous denunciation, and establishes that if Dunbar ever changes his tune, it will be, not because the court has improved, but because Dunbar has been corrupted. The king's gifts are no more than 'tryackill', a word which Professor Kinsley glosses as 'medicine for venomous bites and malignant diseases'. The malignant disease which afflicts Dunbar is the ability to see the truth.

Not many poets exhibit a control of structure and irony equal to that of Dunbar in 'Remonstrance to the King'. The nearest parallel which occurs to me is Horace's dialogue between Ulysses and Tiresias (*Satires* II. v.) on the art of the *captator,* the fortune hunter. This satire is often described as the one in which Horace most nearly approaches the manner of Juvenal. It is in relation to Horace (the *Odes* as well as the *Satires*) and to Juvenal that Dunbar's participation in the northern Renaissance must be judged.

In defiance of chronology, I have begun with Dunbar, partly because he comes closest to the central courtly tradition, partly because he is the best known of the Scottish Renaissance poets. Indeed, with the exception of Burns and McDiarmid, he is probably the best known of all Scottish poets. This pre-eminence has resulted in some injustice to other poets of the period, and in particular to the greatest of them all, Robert Henryson. Dunbar's metrical and linguistic virtuosity, the total effectiveness of his best poems, has to some extent obscured his emotional and intellectual limitations. He misses the two great literary kinds, tragedy and the comedy which depends on interplay of personality and social level, at least partly because he possesses no extensive coherent body of general principles and ideas from which his poetry may grow. Henryson's virtuosity with language and metre is less ostentatious than Dunbar's, and so to some extent has passed unnoticed. His greatness is most plainly to be seen in the range of general principles and ideas which informs his poetry and allows it to encompass tragedy and comedy alike. Henryson is more Shakespearian than Dunbar.

Henryson's comedy and tragedy are both represented in this collection — comedy by the linked series of beast fables which George Bannatyne called *The Tod*; tragedy by *The Testament of Cresseid*. Because the stylistic and other differences between the two are self-evident, I intend to limit the present discussion to the rather less obvious similarities and parallelisms.

Although we know little about Henryson's career, the fact that he was a canon and civil lawyer has been established in terms partly of the records, partly of the references to legal points and procedures which abound in his works. In one sense, then, Henryson possessed a legal mind. It was not, however, a mind limited to points of law and procedure. Equity rather than statute law was his major concern — a concern which merged inevitably into problems of natural and divine law, more especially the relationship between apparent anarchy in the world of human beings, the harsh inevitability of the material creation, and divine authority and mercy. It is here that *The Testament* and *The Tod* are linked.

The central episode of *The Testament* is the trial of

INTRODUCTION

Cresseid before the planetary assembly. The charge, 'sclander and defame injurious', is laid by Cupid before the king, Phoebus, in his parliament, of which Mercury is 'foirspeikar'. The action is not contested. Saturn and Cynthia are made assessors to judge the penalty appropriate to the crime, and it is Cynthia who pronounces the 'sentence diffinityve'. The planets are the powers which govern the material creation, and their sentence, which is in strict accord with the laws of the material universe, transforms Cresseid's entire physical being, and apparently condemns her beyond redemption.

So far as it goes, the legal procedure is incontestable. At the same time, it misses everything which a court of celestial equity might reasonably consider as part of Cresseid's defence, and which Henryson takes good care to keep before the reader's attention. In Henryson, as in Chaucer, Cresseid is an attractive figure whose downfall has been caused as much by circumstance as by personal weakness. She is not the natural wanton of popular tradition:

> *Yit nevertheless quhat ever men deme or say*
> *in scornefull langage of thy brukkilnes,*
> *I sall excuse, als far furth as I may,*
> *thy womanheid, thy wisdome and fairnes:*
> *the quhilk Fortoun hes put to sic distres*
> *as hir pleisit, and nathing throw the gilt*
> *of thee, throw wickit langage to be spilt.*

Henryson comments only on the element of accident which plays so important a part in the establishment of

[19]

popular reputation or infamy. 'Nathing throw the gilt of thee' is the emotional exaggeration of a defence counsel, but it is exaggeration of a truth which the planetary court ignores.

The court also ignores the power over 'all thing generabill' held by its own members. Henryson's planets are the astrological forces which govern human activity so far as that does not result from divine intervention or the exercise of human free will. In particular, planetary action caused the rain which brought Troilus and Cresseid to the first consummation of their love, and planetary action afterwards forced Cresseid into Diomeid's power. The planets themselves, in other words, have caused the circumstances which led to Cresseid's downfall, and they also form the court which judges her consequent blasphemy — not the most equitable situation for a defendant. Such questions leave them unaffected:

> O cruell Saturne! fraward and angrie,
> hard is thy dome, and too malitious;
> on fair Cresseid quhy hes thou na mercie,
> quhilk was sa sweit, gentill and amorous?
> Withdraw thy sentence and be gracious
> as thou was never; so schawis thou thy deid,
> ane wraikfull sentence gevin on fair Cresseid.

In two ways only the situation remains outside planetary control. Cresseid possesses free will, which is capable of rising superior to astral determinism. The planets are not the ultimate authorities of the universe, but are the powerful instruments through which divine

INTRODUCTION

providence may fulfil itself, and which it may on occasion transcend. In the 'spittaill hous', Cresseid does not fall into despair, but by the exercise of free will teaches herself to accept the 'law of lipper leid'. Providence intervenes in Troilus' disinterested act of charity, which causes Cresseid to accept the responsibility for her own deeds, which she had previously refused to acknowledge. Henryson allows no relaxation of the physical punishment for her weakness, but the reader finds in her death after suffering the sense of justice and redemption which marks high tragedy. The action lends itself to Aristotelian analysis, moving us, as it does, to pity and terror — pity for Cresseid herself, terror at the powers she roused against herself — and by way of the peripeteia of Troilus's intervention, producing catharsis at the end.

The ostensible world of *The Testament* is pre-Christian, and divine justice in the context of paganism is the over-all theme. *The Tod* deals with divine and human justice in the declared context of medieval Christianity and at the lower level appropriate to comedy. In terms of plot, it is important to realise that each of the main characters suffers in precise accordance with his deserts. Measure for Measure is as important a theme for Henryson as for Shakespeare. Every major character in *The Tod* bears a precise responsibility for his own misfortunes — Chanteclere and the wolf pay the penalty for allowing themselves to be blinded by self-conceit and flattery; the elder fox failed to keep the terms of his penance; the younger broke the king's peace by killing a lamb. Admiration for the foxes' cleverness is counter-balanced by the helplessness of their victims — 'a littill kid' and the fattest of 'a trip of lambis dansand on a dike'. The stupidity as well as the cleverness of the foxes is emphasised — one stroking his belly as he basks in the sun, and saying

> *Upoun this bellye ware sett a bolt full mete;*

the other forgetting himself a few moments after quoting the very apposite proverb, *felix quem faciunt aliena pericula cautum*. For the foxes in particular there is no possibility of urging mitigating circumstances. Their punishment exemplifies both divine and human justice.

In *The Testament* the retributory aspect of divine justice is symbolised by the planets, and at the same time it is linked to human justice by the concept of a high court, a parliament, of the planets. Henryson, in other words, separates ultimate divine mercy from planetary retributory justice, and more or less equates the latter with human justice. In *The Tod* the same elements combine somewhat differently. The planetary powers return in the second episode:

> *Than Saturne alde was enterit in Capricorne*
> *and Jupiter movit in Sigittarye*
> *and Mars up in the Rammys hede was borne*
> *and Phebus in the Lyoun furth coud carye,*
> *Venus the Crab, the Mone was in Aquarye,*
> *Mercurius, the god of eloquence,*
> *into the Virgin maid his residence.*

These however are not the terrifying deities of *The Testament*: Lourence sees merely

INTRODUCTION

the twinkling sternis clere
and all the planetis of the firmament.

They are powerful, but not merely retributory — Jupiter, for instance, in his house of Sagittarius is particularly favourable, as is Mercury in his exaltation in Virgo. These partly compensate for the adverse power of the Lord of the Ascendent, Saturn, the Greater Infortune, in his house of Capricorn. The planets, all this is to say, do not simply condemn Lourence as they did Cresseid; the universe is a Christian one, and the possibility of redemption remains evidently open in a way not possible for Cresseid. It is for this reason that the fox seeks a confessor. Had he been able to keep the very modest penance imposed by Friar Wolf Waitskath, he might have won his own salvation. His behaviour, however, left him open to the more malignant heavenly influences, and he was killed in the full enjoyment of his sin.

The universe of the poem is Christian; the animals who inhabit it are types of fallen man. Human justice, represented by the lion and his court, the parliament of four-footed beasts, is as fallible as the individual animals, a fact seen most clearly in the relationship of the court to the 'gray stude meir' who refuses to attend the assembly. Here, as usually in Henryson, it is essential to take the *Moralitas* into consideration:

> *This mere is men of contemplatioun,*
> *off pennance walkand in this wildernace,*
> *as monkis and othir men of religioun*
> *that presis God to pleis in every place,*

abstrackit fra this warldis wretchidnes,
in wilful povertee fra pomp and pride,
and fra this warld in mind ar mortifyde.

Clearly the mare's refusal to attend is entirely proper and praiseworthy. It is equally clear, even to the fox, that the primary function of the court should be to suppress such wrongdoers as Fader wer himself:

I wait this suddane semblay that I se,
havand the poyntis of a parliament,
is maid to mar sic misdoaris as me.

The court however makes Fader wer its emissary to force the gray mare, whom it considers contumacious, to compear. When eventually the fox does pay the extreme penalty, it is not for his life of crime, but for an act of lese-majesty, the stupidity of which he should himself have been the first to realise.

The Tod thus establishes an over-all satiric contrast between the fits and starts of human justice (indeed of human activity in general) and the equitable operation of providence as revealed through the stars. Henryson puts the contrast into a specifically Scottish context. The lion, the king of beasts, is the heraldic emblem of the King of Scotland, and when he says:

I lat you wit my mycht is merceabill
and steris none that ar to me prostrat,

he is quoting the Scottish regal motto, *parcere prostratis scit nobilis ira leonis.* (His name, Nobill, derives from the French beast-epic, but also refers to the same motto.) It is a nice touch that the servants who carry his crown are the three heraldic leopards of England. Unicorn Pursuivant, one of the Scottish college of heralds, makes the proclamation summoning the parliament. The king's peace is proclaimed, the court is fenced, justice and doomster are present, in full accord with Scottish procedure for holding justice ayres, assize courts, in the presence of the king.

The gray mare represents 'men of contemplatioun'; the central point of the satire is that the Scottish crown and parliament make a presumptious and unsuccessful attempt to establish their authority in spiritual as well as temporal matters. The conflict is not simply between state and church. Some churchmen — for example, the wolf who 'hes the practik of the chancellary' and represents the type of ecclesiastic who becomes a senior civil servant — have given themselves over to the secular interest. The primary reference is to 'monkis and othir men of religioun' — the enclosed orders — and in this context Henryson's association with the Benedictine abbey of Dunfermline should not be forgotten. In the late sixteenth century, the Roman Catholic historian, John Leslie, Bishop of Ross, traced the origin of religious strife in Scotland to the year 1468 when James III intruded Henry Crichton as abbot of Dunfermline in place of Alexander Thomson who had been duly elected by the monks.

Henryson, it is probably fair to say, recognises the contemplative life as the summit of human existence and achievement, without in the least blinding himself to the

many unsatisfactory aspects of the religious life of Scotland
and Europe in his time. One of those was certainly the
encroachment of secular power, not only externally from
the king and parliament, but internally from the ambitions
of secularized clerics of the type represented by the wolf-
ambassador. Nor was secularization the only danger. The
contrast between the gray mare and the wolf-ambassador
is no more striking than that between the gray mare and
Frere Wolf Waitskath. Lourence might have escaped his
destiny if he had kept to the light penance which the
friar imposed on him, but the friar's administration of the
sacrament of penance remains woefully inadequate.
(Again, one should recollect that Henryson's personal
connections were with monks; he always treats friars in
a rather unfriendly spirit.)

Elsewhere I have remarked that the critics who find a
foretaste of Calvinism in Henryson are deluding them-
selves, a position to which I still hold. Henryson had no
prophetic powers. But he did have a very clear eye for the
religious situation of his own day and, by the power of
hindsight, it is possible for us to see at least the social
origins of the Reformation in the world of the poem.

Henryson and Dunbar nowhere attempted to visualize
a society radically different from the one known to them.
With many incidental reservations, they accepted an order
based on the monarchy and the medieval church. On
Church matters, Lindsay is more revolutionary than his
predecessors, but he does not essentially differ from them
in his attitude to the monarchy. Long before his death,
in or about 1555, however, the monarchy must have

become subject to questioning almost as searching as that applied to the church, a questioning which was to bear later fruit in the *De Jure Regni apud Scottos* (1579) of George Buchanan, in the doctrine of the Two Kingdoms, the church and the state, promulgated by Andrew Melville (1545-1622), and still later in the National Covenant of 1638, the Solemn League and Covenant of 1643, and the extreme doctrines of the Cameronians towards the end of the seventeenth century. Nevertheless, it is clear that when in 1560 the Reformation overthrew one pillar of the old order, the other, the monarchy, became the central hope of many who, in Alexander Scott's phrase, wished 'to temper time with trew con-tinuance'. Their hopes cannot have been overstrong — with the disadvantages of womanhood, Mary combined those of Roman Catholicism and a French background and upbringing — but they were sincere, and explain some of the loyalty to Mary which survived even her most aberrant behaviour. Later monarchs, Charles I and II and James VII, were to receive a similiar loyalty for a similar reason — but from an increasingly small pro-portion of the population. Alexander Scott's *Ane New Yeir Gift to the Quene Mary, quhen scho come first Hame, 1562,* is the most memorable expression of moderate hopes before the medieval world-order began its final dis-appearance.

ROBERT HENRYSON
(c. 1420–c. 1490)

I

The Annunciation

1

Forcy as deith is likand lufe
throuch quhome al bittir swet is.
No thing is hard, as writ can pruf,
till him in lufe that letis.
Luf us fra barret betis,
quhen fra the hevinly sete abufe
in message Gabriell couth muf
and with mild Mary metis
and said, 'God wele thee gretis.
In thee he will tak rest and rufe
but hurt of syne or yit reprufe.
In him sett thy decreit is.'

2

This message mervale gert that mild
and silence held but soundis,
as weill aferit a maid infild.
The angell it expoundis

how that hir wame but woundis
consave it suld, fra syne exild,
and quhen this carpin wes compilit,
brichtnes fra bufe aboundis.
than fell that gay to groundis;
of Goddis grace na thing begild,
wox in hir chaumer chaist with child,
with Christ, our king that cround is.

3

Thir tithingis tauld, the messinger
till hevin agane he glidis.
That princess pure withoutyn peir
full plesandly applidis
and blith with barne abidis.
O worthy wirschip singuler
to be moder and madyn meir,
as Cristin faith confidis,
that borne was of hir sidis
our Maker, Goddis sone so deir,
quhilk erd, wattir and hevinnis cler
throw grace and virtu gidis!

4

The miraclis ar mekle and meit
fra luffis river rynnis:
the low of luf haldand the hete
unbrynt full blithlie birnis:

quhen Gabriell beginnis
with mouth that gudely may to grete,
the wand of Aarone, dry but wete,
to burioun nocht blynnis:
the flesch all donk within is:
upone the erd na drop couth fleit:
sa was that may maid moder swete
and sakeles of all synnis.

5

Hir mervalus haill madinhede
God in hir bosum bracis
and hir divinite fra dreid
hir kepit in all casis.
The hie God of his gracis
him self dispisit us to speid
and dowtit nocht to dee one deid.
He panit for our peacis
and with his blude us bacis,
bot quhen he ras up, as we rede,
the cherite of his Godhede
was plane in every place is.

6

O lady lele and lusumest,
thy face moist fair and schene is!
O lady blithe and bowsumest,
fra carnale crime that clene is,

this prayer fra my splene is,
that all my werkis wikkitest
thou put away and mak me chaist
fra Termigant that teyne is
and fra his cluke that kene is
and syne till hevin my saule thou haist
quhar thy Makar of michtis mast
is King and thou thair Quene is.

II

The Testament of Cresseid

Ane doolie sessoun to ane cairfull dyte
suld correspond, and be equivalent.
Richt sa it wes quhen I began to wryte
this tragedie, the wedder richt fervent,
quhen Aries, in middis of the Lent,
schouris of haill can fra the north discend,
that scantlie fra the cauld I micht defend.

Yit nevertheles within myne oratur
I stude, quhen Titan had his bemis bricht
withdrawin doun, and sylit under cure
and fair Venus, the bewtie of the nicht,
uprais, and set unto the west full richt
hir goldin face in oppositioun
of God Phebus direct discending doun.

[32]

Throw out the glas hir bemis brast sa fair
that I micht se on everie syde me by
the Northin wind had purifyit the Air
and sched the mistie cloudis fra the sky,
the froist freisit, the blastis bitterly
fra Pole Artick come quhisling loud and schill,
and causit me remufe aganis my will.

For I traistit that Venus, luifis Quene,
to quhome sum tyme I hecht obedience,
my faidit hart of lufe scho wald mak grene,
and therupon with humbill reverence,
I thocht to pray hir hie Magnificence;
bot for greit cald as than I lattit was,
and in my Chalmer to the fyre can pas.

Thocht lufe be hait, yit in ane man of age
it kendillis nocht sa sone as in youtheid,
of quhome the blude is flowing in ane rage,
and in the auld the curage doif and deid,
of quhilk the fyre outward is best remeid;
to help be Phisike quhair that nature faillit
I am expert, for baith I have assailit.

I mend the fyre and beikit me about,
than tuik ane drink my spreitis to comfort,
and armit me weill fra the cauld thairout:
to cut the winter nicht and mak it schort,
I tuik ane Quair, and left all uther sport,
writtin be worthie Chaucer glorious,
of fair Creisseid, and worthie Troylus.

And thair I fand, efter that Diomeid
ressavit had that Lady bricht of hew,
how Troilus neir out of wit abraid,
and weipit soir with visage paill of hew;
for quhilk wanhope his teiris can renew
quhil Esperus rejoisit him agane,
Thus quhyle in Joy he levit, quhyle in pane.

Of hir behest he had greit comforting,
traisting to Troy that scho suld mak retour,
quhilk he desyrit maist of eirdly thing
forquhy scho was his only Paramour;
bot quhen he saw passit baith day and hour
of hir ganecome, than sorrow can oppres
his wofull hart in cair and hevines.

Of his distres me neidis nocht reheirs,
for worthie Chauceir in the samin buik
in gudelie termis and in Joly veirs
compylit hes his cairis, quha will luik.
To brek my sleip ane uther quair I tuik,
in quhilk I fand the fatall destenie
of fair Cresseid, that endit wretchitlie.

Quha wait gif all that Chauceir wrait was trew?
Nor I wait nocht gif this narratioun
be authoreist, or fenyeit of the new
be sum Poeit, throw his Inventioun,
maid to report the Lamentatioun
and wofull end of this lustie Cresseid,
and quhat distres scho thoillit, and quhat deid.

2

Quhen Diomeid had all his appetyte, / *doded*.
and mair, fulfillit of this fair Ladie,
upon ane uther he set his haill delyte
and send to hir ane Lybell of repudie,
and hir excludit fra his companie.
Than desolait scho walkit up and doun,
and sum men sayis into the Court commoun.

O fair Creisseid, the flour and A per se
of Troy and Grece, how was thou fortunait!
to change in filth all thy Feminitie,
and be with fleschlie lust sa maculait,
and go amang the Greikis air and lait
sa giglotlike, takand thy foull plesance!
I have pietie thou suld fall sic mischance.

Yit nevertheless quhat ever men deme or say
in scornefull langage of thy brukkilnes,
I sall excuse, als far furth as I may,
thy womanheid, thy wisdome and fairnes:
the quhilk Fortoun hes put to sic distres
as hir pleisit, and nathing throw the gilt
of thee, throw wickit langage to be spilt.

This fair Lady, in this wyse destitute
of all comfort and consolatioun,
richt privelie, but fellowschip, on fute
disagysit passit far out of the toun
ane myle or twa, unto ane Mansioun
beildit full gay, quhair hir father Calchas
quhilk than amang the Greikis dwelland was.

[35]

Quhen he hir saw, the caus he can Inquyre
of hir cumming; scho said, siching full soir:
'Fra Diomeid had gottin his desyre
he wox werie, and wald of me no moir.'
Quod Calchas, 'douchter, weip thou not thairfoir;
peraventure all cummis for the best;
welcum to me, thou art full deir ane Gest.'

This auld Calchas, efter the Law was tho,
wes keiper of the Tempill as ane Preist,
in quhilk Venus and hir Sone Cupido
war honourit, and his Chalmer was thame neist,
to quhilk Cresseid with baill aneuch in breist
usit to pas, hir prayeris for to say.
Quhill at the last, upon ane Solempne day,

as custome was, the pepill far and neir
befoir the none, unto the Tempill went,
with Sacrifice, devoit in thair maneir:
bot still Cresseid, hevie in hir Intent,
into the Kirk wald not hir self present,
for giving of the pepill ony deming
of hir expuls fra Diomeid the King:

bot past into ane secreit Orature
quhair scho micht weip hir wofull desteny;
behind hir bak scho cloisit fast the dure
and on hir kneis bair fell doun in hy.
Upon Venus and Cupide angerly
scho cryit out, and said on this same wyse,
'Allace that ever I maid you Sacrifice.

3 'Ye gave me anis ane devine responsaill
that I suld be the flour of luif in Troy,
now am I maid ane unworthie outwaill,
and all in cair translatit is my Joy;
quha sall me gyde? quha sall me now convoy
sen I fra Diomeid and Nobill Troylus
am clene excludit, as abject odious?

'O fals Cupide, is nane to wyte bot thow,
and thy Mother, of lufe the blind Goddes!
Ye causit me alwayis understand and trow
the seid of lufe was sawin in my face,
and ay grew grene throw your supplie and grace.
Bot now allace that seid with froist is slane,
and I fra luifferis left and all forlane.'

4 Quhen this was said, doun in ane extasie,
ravischit in spreit, intill ane dreame scho fell,
and be apperance hard, quhair scho did ly,
Cupide the King ringand ane silver bell,
quhilk men micht heir fra hevin unto hell;
at quhais sound befoir Cupide appeiris
the seven Planetis discending fra thair Spheiris,

quhilk hes power of all thing generabill
to reull and steir be thair greit Influence,
wedder and wind, and coursis variabill:
and first of all Saturne gave his sentence,
quhilk gave to Cupide litill reverence,
Bot, as ane busteous Churle on his maneir,
Come crabitlie with auster luik and cheir.

His face fronsit, his lyre was lyke the Leid,
his teith chatterit, and cheverit with the Chin,
his Ene drowpit, how sonkin in his heid,
out of his Nois the Meldrop fast can rin,
with lippis bla and cheikis leine and thin;
the Iceschoklis that fra his hair doun hang
was wonder greit, and as ane speir als lang.

Atouir his belt his lyart lokkis lay
felterit unfair, ouirfret with Froistis hoir;
his garmound and his gyis full gay of gray,
his widderit weid fra him the wind out woir;
ane busteous bow within his hand he boir;
under his girdill ane flasche of felloun flanis,
fedderit with Ice, and heidit with hailstanis.

Than Juppiter, richt fair and amiabill,
God of the Starnis in the Firmament,
and Nureis to all thing generabill,
fra his Father Saturne far different,
with burelie face, and browis bricht and brent,
upon his heid ane Garland, wonder gay,
of flouris fair, as it had bene in May.

His voice was cleir, as Cristall wer his Ene,
as goldin wyre sa glitterand was his hair;
his garmound and his gyis full gay of grene,
with golden listis gilt on everie gair;
ane burelie brand about his midill bair;
in his richt hand he had ane groundin speir,
of his Father the wraith fra us to weir.

Nixt efter him come Mars, the God of Ire,
of strife, debait, and all dissensioun,
to chide and fecht, als feirs as ony fyre;
in hard Harnes, hewmound and Habirgeoun,
and on his hanche ane roustie fell Fachioun;
and in his hand he had ane roustie sword;
wrything his face with mony angrie word,

Schaikand his sword, befoir Cupide he come
with reid visage, and grislie glowrand Ene;
and at his mouth ane bullar stude of fome
lyke to ane Bair quhetting his Tuskis kene,
richt Tuitlyeour lyke, but temperance in tene;
ane horne he blew, with mony bosteous brag,
quhilk all this warld with weir hes maid to wag.

Than fair Phebus, Lanterne & Lamp of licht
of man and beist, baith frute and flourisching,
Tender Nureis, and banischer of nicht,
and of the warld causing, be his moving
and Influence, lyfe in all eirdlie thing,
without comfort of quhome, of force to nocht
must all ga die that in this warld is wrocht.

As King Royall he raid upon his Chair
the quhilk Phaeton gydit sum tyme upricht;
the brichtnes of his face quhen it was bair
nane micht behald for peirsing of his sicht.
This goldin Cart with fyrie bemis bricht
four yokkit steidis full different of hew,
but bait or tyring, throw the Spheiris drew.

The first was soyr, with Mane als reid as Rois,
callit Eoye into the Orient;
the secund steid to Name hecht Ethios,
quhitlie and paill, and sum deill ascendent;
the thrid Peros, richt hait and richt fervent:
the feird was blak, callit Philologie
quhilk rollis Phebus doun into the sey.

Venus was thair present that goddes gay,
hir Sonnis querrell for to defend and mak
hir awin complaint, cled in ane nyce array,
the ane half grene, the uther half Sabill black;
quhyte hair as gold kemmit and sched abak;
bot in hir face semit greit variance,
quhyles perfyte treuth, and quhyles Inconstance.

Under smyling scho was dissimulait,
provocative, with blenkis Amorous,
and suddanely changit and alterait,
angrie as ony Serpent vennemous
richt pungitive, with wordis odious.
Thus variant scho was, quha list tak keip,
with ane Eye lauch, and with the uther weip,

In taikning that all fleschelie Paramour
quhilk Venus hes in reull and governance,
is sum tyme sweit, sum tyme bitter and sour
richt unstabill, and full of variance,
mingit with cairful Joy and fals plesance,
now hait, now cauld, now blyith, now full of wo,
now grene as leif, now widderit and ago.

ROBERT HENRYSON

With buik in hand than come Mercurius,
richt Eloquent, and full of Rethorie,
with polite termis and delicious,
with pen and Ink to report al reddie,
setting sangis and singand merilie:
his Hude was reid, heklit atouir his Croun,
lyke to ane Poeit of the auld fassoun.

Boxis he bair with fine Electuairis,
and sugerit Syropis for digestioun,
spycis belangand to the Pothecairis,
with mony hailsum sweit Confectioun,
doctour in Phisick cled in ane Skarlot goun,
and furrit weill, as sic ane aucht to be,
honest and gude, and not ane word culd le.

Nixt efter him come Lady Cynthia,
the last of all, and swiftest in hir Spheir,
of colour blak, buskit with hornis twa,
and in the nicht scho listis best appeir.
haw as the Leid, of colour nathing cleir;
for all hir licht scho borrowis at hir brother
Titan, for of hir self scho hes nane uther.

Hir gyse was gray, and ful of spottis blak,
and on hir breist ane Churle paintit full evin,
beirand ane bunche of Thornis on his bak,
quhilk for his thift micht clim na nar the hevin.
Thus quhen thay gadderit war, thir Goddes sevin,
Mercurius thay cheisit with ane assent
to be foirspeikar in the Parliament.

Quha had bene thair, and liken for to heir
his facound toung, and termis exquisite,
of Rethorick the prettick he micht leir,
in breif Sermone ane pregnant sentence wryte:
befoir Cupide veiling his Cap alyte,
speiris the caus of that vocatioun,
and he anone schew his Intentioun.

5 'Lo!' (quod Cupide), 'quha will blaspheme the name
of his awin God, outher in word or deid,
to all Goddis he dois baith lak and schame,
and suld have bitter panis to his meid.
I say this by yone wretchit Cresseid,
the quilk throw me was sum tyme flour of lufe,
me and my Mother starklie can reprufe.

'Saying of hir greit Infelicitie
I was the caus, and my Mother Venus,
ane blind Goddes, hir cald, that micht not se,
with sclander and defame Injurious;
thus hir leving unclene and Lecherous
scho wald returne on me and my Mother,
to quhome I schew my grace abone all uther.

'And sen ye ar all sevin deificait,
participant of devyne sapience,
this greit Injurie done to our hie estait
me think with pane we suld mak recompence;
was never to Goddes done sic violence.
Asweill for yow, as for myself I say;
thairfoir ga help to revenge I yow pray.'

[42]

Mercurius to Cupide gave answeir
and said: 'Schir King my counsall is that ye
refer yow to the hiest planeit heir,
and tak to him the lawest of degre,
the pane of Cresseid for to modifie;
as god Saturne, with him tak Cynthia.'
'I am content' (quod he) 'to tak thay twa.'

Than thus proceidit Saturne and the Mone,
quhen thay the mater rypelie had degest,
for the dispyte to Cupide scho had done,
and to Venus oppin and manifest,
in all hir lyfe with pane to be opprest,
and torment sair, with seiknes Incurabill,
and to all lovers be abhominabill.

This duleful sentence Saturne tuik on hand,
and passit doun quhair cairfull Cresseid lay,
and on hir heid he laid ane frostie wand;
than lawfullie on this wyse can he say:
'Thy greit fairnes and all thy bewtie gay,
thy wantoun blude, and eik thy goldin Hair,
heir I exclude fra the for evermair.

'I change thy mirth into Melancholy,
quhilk is the Mother of all pensivenes;
thy Moisture and thy heit in cald and dry;
thyne Insolence, thy play and wantones
to greit diseis; thy Pomp and thy riches
in mortall neid; and greit penuritie
thou suffer sall, and as ane beggar die.'

O cruell Saturne! fraward and angrie,
hard is thy dome, and too malitious;
on fair Cresseid quhy hes thou na mercie,
quhilk was sa sweit, gentill and amorous?
Withdraw thy sentence and be gracious
as thou was never; so schawis thow thy deid,
ane wraikfull sentence gevin on fair Cresseid.

Than Cynthia, quhen Saturne past away,
out of hir sait discendit doun belyve,
and red ane bill on Cresseid quhair scho lay,
contening this sentence diffinityve:
'Fra heit of bodie I the now depryve,
and to thy seiknes sal be na recure,
bot in dolour thy dayis to Indure.

'Thy Cristall Ene minglit with blude I mak,
thy voice sa cleir, unplesand hoir and hace,
thy lustie lyre ouirspred with spottis blak,
and lumpis haw appeirand in thy face.
Quhair thou cumis, Ilk man sal fle the place.
This sall thou go begging fra hous to hous
with Cop and Clapper lyke ane Lazarous.'

This doolie dreame, this uglye visioun
brocht to ane end, Cresseid fra it awoik,
and all that Court and convocatioun
vanischit away, than rais scho up and tuik
ane poleist glas, and hir schaddow culd luik:
and quhen scho saw hir face sa deformait
gif scho in hart was wa aneuch God wait.

Weiping full sair, 'Lo quhat it is' (quod sche)
'with fraward langage for to muse and steir
our craibit Goddis, and sa is sene on me!
My blaspheming now have I bocht full deir.
All eirdlie Joy and mirth I set areir.
Allace this day, allace this wofull tyde,
quhen I began with my Goddis for to Chyde.'

Be this was said ane Chyld come fra the Hall
to warne Cresseid the Supper was reddy,
first knokkit at the dure, and syne culd call:
'Madame your Father biddis yow cum in hy.
He hes mervell sa lang on grouf ye ly,
and sayis your prayers bene to lang sum deill:
the goddis wait all your Intent full weill.'

Quod scho: 'Fair Chyld ga to my Father deir,
and pray him cum to speik with me anone.'
And sa he did, and said: 'douchter quhat cheir?'
'Allace' (quod scho) 'Father, my mirth is gone.'
'Allace' (quod he); and scho can all expone
as I have tauld, the vengeance and the wraik
for hir trespas, Cupide on hir culd tak.

He luikit on hir uglye Lipper face,
the quhilk before was quhyte as Lillie flour;
wringand his handis oftymes he said allace
that he had levit to se that wofull hour,
for he knew weill that thair was na succour
to hir seiknes, and that dowblit his pane.
Thus was thair cair aneuch betuix thame twane.

[45]

Quhen thay togidder murnit had full lang,
quod Cresseid: 'Father, I wald not be kend.
Thairfoir in secreit wyse ye let me gang
into yone Hospitall at the tounis end,
and thidder sum meit for Cheritie me send
to leif upon, for all mirth in this eird
is fra me gane, sic is my wickit weird.'

Than in ane Mantill and ane bawer Hat,
with Cop and Clapper wonder prively,
he opnit ane secreit yet, and out thair at
convoyit hir, that na man suld espy,
into ane Village half ane myle thairby,
delyverit hir in at the Spittaill hous,
and daylie sent hir part of his Almous.

Sum knew her weill, & sum had na knawledge
of hir becaus scho was sa deformait,
with bylis blak ouirspred in hir visage,
and hir fair colour faidit and alterait.
Yit thay presumit for her hie regrait
and still murning, scho was of Nobill kin:
with better will thairfoir they tuik hir in.

The day passit, and Phebus went to rest,
the Cloudis blak ouirquhelmit all the sky.
God wait gif Cresseid was ane sorrowfull Gest,
seing that uncouth fair and Harbery:
but meit or drink scho dressit hir to ly
in ane dark Corner of the Hous allone,
and on this wyse weiping, scho maid her mone:

[46]

ROBERT HENRYSON

The Complaint of Cresseid

'O sop of sorrow, sonkin into cair:
O Cative Creisseid, for now and ever mair,
gane is thy Joy and all thy mirth in Eird,
of all blyithnes now art thou blaiknit bair.
Thair is na Salve may saif the of thy sair,
fell is thy Fortoun, wickit is thy weird:
thy blyis is baneist, and thy baill on breird;
under the Eirth, God gif I gravin wer,
quhair nane of Grece not yit of Troy micht heird.

'Quhair is thy Chalmer wantounlie besene?
with burely bed and bankouris browderit bene,
spycis and Wyne to thy Collatioun,
the Cowpis all of gold and silver schene:
the sweit Meitis, servit in plaittis clene,
with Saipheron sals of ane gud sessoun:
thy gay garmentis with mony gudely Goun,
thy plesand Lawn pinnit with goldin prene:
all is areir, thy greit Royall Renoun.

'Quhair is thy garding with thir greissis gay?
and fresche flowris, quhilk the Quene Floray
had paintit plesandly in everie pane,
quhair thou was wont full merilye in May
to walk and tak the dew be it was day
and heir the Merle and Mawis mony ane,

[47]

with Ladyis fair in Carrolling to gane,
and se the Royall Rinkis in thair array,
in garmentis gay garnischit on everie grane.

'Thy greit triumphand fame and hie honour,
quhair thou was callit of Eirdlye wichtis Flour,
all is decayit, thy weird is welterit so.
Thy hie estait is turnit in darknes dour.
This Lipper Ludge tak for thy burelie Bour,
and for thy Bed tak now ane bunche of stro;
for waillit Wyne, and Meitis thou had tho,
tak mowlit Breid, Peirrie and Ceder sour:
bot Cop and Clapper, now is all ago.

'My cleir voice, and courtlie carrolling,
quhair I was wont with Ladyis for to sing,
is rawk as Ruik, full hiddeous hoir and hace;
my plesand port all utheris precelling—
of lustines I was hald maist conding—
now is deformit: the Figour of my face,
to luik on it, na Leid now lyking hes:
sowpit in syte, I say with sair siching,
ludgeit amang the Lipper Leid allace.

'O Ladyis fair of Troy and Grece, attend
my miserie, quhilk nane may comprehend,
my frivoll Fortoun, my Infelicitie,
my greit mischeif quhilk na man can amend.
Be war in tyme, approchis neir the end,
and in your mynd ane mirrour mak of me:

[48]

as I am now, peradventure that ye
for all your micht may cum to that same end,
or ellis war, gif ony war may be.

'Nocht is your fairnes bot ane faiding flour,
nocht is your famous laud and hie honour
bot wind Inflat in uther mennis eiris.
Your roising reid to rotting sall retour:
exempill mak of me in your Memour,
quhilk of sic thingis wofull witnes beiris,
all Welth in Eird, away as Wind it weiris.
Be war thairfoir, approchis neir the hour:
Fortoun is fikkill, quhen scho beginnis & steiris.'

Thus chydand with hir drerie destenye,
weiping, scho woik the nicht fra end to end,
bot all in vane; hir dule, hir cairfull cry
micht not remeid, nor yit hir murning mend.
Ane Lipper Lady rais and till hir wend,
and said: 'quhy spurnis thow aganis the Wall,
to sla thy self, and mend nathing at all?

'Sen thy weiping dowbillis bot thy wo,
I counsall the mak vertew of ane neid,
to leir to clap thy Clapper to and fro,
and leir efter the Law of Lipper Leid.'
Thair was na buit, bot furth with thame scho yeid,
fra place to place, quhill cauld and hounger sair
compellit hir to be ane rank beggair.

ROBERT HENRYSON

That samin tyme of Troy the Garnisoun,
quhilk had to chiftane worthie Troylus,
throw Jeopardie of Weir had strikken doun
knichtis of Grece in number mervellous;
with greit tryumphe and Laude victorious
agane to Troy richt Royallie they raid
the way quhair Cresseid with the Lipper baid.

Seeing that companie thai come all with ane stevin;
thay gaif ane cry and schuik coppis gude speid,
said 'worthie Lordis for goddis lufe of Hevin,
to us Lipper part of your Almous deid.'
Than to thair cry Nobill Troylus tuik heid,
having pietie, neir by the place can pas,
quhair Cresseid sat, not witting quhat scho was.

Than upon him scho kest up baith hir Ene,
and with ane blenk it come into his thocht,
that he sumtime hir face befoir had sene,
bot scho was in sic plye he knew hir nocht;
yit than hir luik into his mynd it brocht
the sweit visage and amorous blenking
of fair Cresseid sumtyme his awin darling.

Na wonder was, suppois in mynd that he
tuik hir figure sa sone, and lo now quhy?
The Idole of ane thing, in cace may be
sa deip Imprentit in the fantasy
that it deludis the wittis outwardly,
and sa appeiris in forme and lyke estait,
within the mynd as it was figurait.

Ane spark of lufe than till his hart culd spring
and kendlit all his bodie in ane fyre.
With hait Fewir ane sweit and trimbling
him tuik, quhill he was reddie to expyre.
To beir his Scheild, his Breist began to tyre;
within ane quhyle he changit mony hew,
and nevertheless not ane ane uther knew.

For Knichtlie pietie and memoriall
of fair Cresseid, ane Gyrdill can he tak,
ane Purs of gold, and mony gay Jowall,
and in the Skirt of Cresseid doun can swak;
than raid away, and not ane word he spak,
pensive in hart, quhill he come to the Toun,
and for greit care oft syis almaist fell doun.

The lipper folk to Cresseid than can draw,
to se the equall distributioun
of the Almous, bot quhen the gold thay saw,
ilk ane to uther prevelie can roun,
and said: 'Yone Lord hes mair affectioun,
how ever it be, unto yone Lazarous
than to us all, we knaw be his Almous.'

'Quhat Lord is yone' (quod scho), 'have ye na feill,
hes done to us so greit humanitie?'
'Yes' (quod a Lipper man), 'I knaw him weill,
Schir Troylus it is, gentill and fre.'
Quhen Cresseid understude that it was he,
stiffer than steill, thair stert ane bitter stound
throwout hir hart, and fell doun to the ground.

Quhen scho ouircome, with siching sair & sad,
with mony cairfull cry and cald ochane:
'Now is my breist with stormie stoundis stad,
wrappit in wo, ane wretch full will of wane.'
Than swounit scho oft or scho culd refrane,
and ever in hir swouning cryit scho thus:
'O fals Cresseid and trew Knicht Troylus.

'Thy lufe, thy lawtie, and thy gentilnes,
I countit small in my prosperitie,
sa elevait I was in wantones,
And clam upon the fickill quheill sa hie:
all Faith and Lufe I promissit to the,
was in the self fickill and frivolous:
O fals Cresseid, and trew Knicht Troilus.

'For lufe of me thou keipt gude continence,
honest and chaist in conversatioun.
Of all wemen protectour and defence
thou was, and helpit thair opinioun.
My mynd in fleschelie foull affectioun
was Inclynit to Lustis Lecherous:
fy fals Cresseid, O trew Knicht Troylus.

'Lovers be war and tak gude heid about
quhome that ye lufe, for quhome ye suffer paine.
I lat yow wit, thair is richt few thairout
quhome ye may traist to have trew lufe agane.
Preif quhen ye will, your labour is in vaine.
Thairfoir, I reid, ye tak thame as ye find,
for thay ar sad as Widdercock in Wind,

'Because I knaw the greit unstabilnes
brukkill as glas, into my self I say,
traisting in uther als greit unfaithfulnes,
Als unconstant, and als untrew of fay,
thocht sum be trew, I wait richt few ar thay:
quha findis treuth lat him his Lady ruse:
nane but my self as now I will accuse.'

Quhen this was said, with Paper scho sat doun,
and on this maneir maid hir Testament.
'Heir I beteiche my Corps and Carioun
with Wormis and with Taidis to be rent.
My Cop and Clapper and myne Ornament,
and all my gold the Lipper folk sall have,
quhen I am deid, to burie me in grave.

'This Royal Ring, set with this Rubie reid,
quhilk Troylus in drowrie to me send,
to him agane I leif it quhen I am deid,
to mak my cairfull deid unto him kend:
thus I conclude schortlie and mak ane end,
my Spreit I leif to Diane quhair scho dwellis,
to walk with hir in waist Woddis and Wellis.

'O Diomeid, thou hes baith Broche and Belt,
quhilk Troylus gave me in takning
of his trew lufe,' and with that word scho swelt,
and sone ane Lipper man tuik of the Ring,
syne buryit hir withouttin tarying:
to Troylus furthwith the Ring he bair,
and of Cresseid the deith he can declair.

Quhen he had hard hir greit infirmitie,
hir Legacie and Lamentatioun,
and how scho endit in sic povertie,
he swelt for wo, and fell doun in ane swoun,
for greit sorrow his hart to brist was boun:
siching full sadlie, said: 'I can no moir,
scho was untrew, and wo is me thairfoir.'

Sum said he maid ane Tomb of Merbell gray,
and wrait hir name and superscriptioun,
and laid it on hir grave quhair that scho lay,
in goldin Letteris, conteining this ressoun:
'Lo, fair Ladyis, Cresseid, of Troyis toun,
sumtyme countit the flour of Womanheid,
under this stane lait Lipper lyis deid.'

Now, worthie Wemen, in this Ballet schort,
made for your worschip and Instructioun,
of Cheritie, I monische and exhort,
ming not your lufe with fals deceptioun.
Beir in your mynd this schort conclusioun
of fair Cresseid, as I have said befoir.
Sen scho is deid, I speik of hir no moir.

Finis.

ROBERT HENRYSON

III
The Tod

1

Thoucht brutale bestis be irrationale,
that is to say, lakking discretioun,
yit ilkane in thair kyndis naturale
hes mony divers inclinatioun —
the bair bustous, the wolf, the wild lyoun,
the fox fenyeit, craftye and cautelous,
the dog to berk in nycht and keip the hous.

2

So different thay bene, in propirteis
unknawin unto man and infinite,
in kind haifand so fele diversiteis
my connyng it excedis for to dyte.
Forthy as now my purpois is to write
a cas I fand quhilk fell this hinder yere
betwix a fox and gentill Chanteclere.

3

A wedow dwelt intill a drope thay dais,
quhilk wan hir fude with spinning on hir rok,
and had no moir guidis, as the fable sais,
except of hennis scho had a lyttill flok,
and thame to kepe scho had a joly cok,
rycht curageous, unto this wedow ay
devidand nycht, crawand befoir the day.

[55]

4

A lytill fra that foirsaid wedois hous
a thorny schaw thair was of grit defence,
quhairin a fox, craftye and cautelous,
maid his repair and daylie residence,
quhilk to this wedow did grete violence
in piking of hir pultry day and nycht,
and be no mene revengit on him scho mycht.

5

This wily tod, quhen that the lark coud sing,
full sare hungrye unto the toun him drest,
quhair Chanteclere into the gray dawing,
wery of nycht, was flowin fra his nest.
Lourence this saw and in his mind he kest
the juperteis, the wayis and the wile
be quhat menis he mycht this cok begile.

6

Dissimuland thus in countenance and chere,
on knees fell and smyland thus he said,
'Gude morne, my maister, gentill Chanteclere!'
With that the cok stert bakward in a braid.
'Schir, be my saull, ye neid nocht be affraid,
nor yit for me to drede nor flee abak —
I come bot here you service for to mak.

7

Wald I nocht serve you, ser, I wer to blame,
as I have done to youre progenitouris.
Your fader oft fulfillit hes my wame

and send me mete fra middingis to the muiris.
At his ending I did my besy curis
To hald his hede and gife him drinkis warme,
syne at the last that swete swelt in my arme.'

8

'Knew thou my fader?' quod the cok and leuch.
'Ya, my fair sone, forsuth I held his hede
quhen that he swelt under a birkyn beuch,
syne said the dirige quhen that he was dede.
Betwix us twa how suld thair be a fede?
Quhom suld ye trest bot me, your servitour,
quhilk to your fader did sa grite honour?

9

Quhen I behald your fetheris fair and gent,
youre breste, your beke, your hekill and your came,
schir, be my saule, and the blissit sacrament,
my hert warmys, me think I am at hame.
You for to serve I wald crepe on my wame
in frost and snaw, in wederis wan and wete,
and lay my lyart lokkis under your fete.'

10

This feynit fox fals and dissimilate
maid to the cok a cavillatioun,
'Me think you changit and degenerate
fra your fader and his conditioun.
Off crafty crawing he mycht bere the croun,
for he wald on his tais stand and crawe.
This is no lee — I stude beside and sawe.'

11

With that the cok upoun his tais hee
kest up his beke and sang with all his mycht.
Quod Lourence than, 'Now, ser, sa mot I thee,
ye ar your faderis sone and air up rycht,
bot yit ye want of his cunning ane slicht.'
'Quhat?' quod the cok, 'He wald, and haif na dout,
bayth wink and craw and turne him thryis about.'

12

Thus inflate with the wind of fals vaine gloir
quhilk puttis monye to confusioun,
trestand to win a grit worschip thairfore,
unwarlye winkand, walkit up and doun,
and syne to chant and craw he maid him boun,
and suddanlie, or he had sung ane note,
the fox was war and hynt him be the throte.

13

Syne to the schaw but tarye with him hyit,
off countermaund haifond bot lytill dout.
With that Sprowtok, Coppok and Partlot cryit.
The wedow hard and with a cry come out.
Seand the cais, scho said and gaif a schout,
'How, murthour, reylock!' with a hiddeous beir,
'Alace! have I now lost guid Chanteclere?'

14

As scho war wod, with monye yell and cry
ryvand hir hair, upoun hir breist can bete:
syne paill of hew, half in ane exstasye,

[58]

fel doun for cair in swoning and in swete.
With that the willye hennis left thair mete,
and quhill this wife was lyand thus in swoun,
fell of that cais in disputatioun.

15

'Alace,' quod Partlot, makand sair murning,
with teiris grete attour hir chekis fell,
'Yone was our drourye and our dayis darling,
oure nychtingale and als our horlage bell,
oure walcryif weche us for to warne and tell
quhen that Aurora with hir curchis gray
put up hir hede betwix the nycht and the day.

16

Quha sall our lemmane be? quha sall us leid?
quhen we ar sad, quha sall unto us sing?
With his sweit bill he wald brek us the breid.
In all this warld was thair na kyndar thing.
In paramouris he wald do us plesing
at his power, as Nature list him gyffe.
Now eftir him, alace, how sall we live?'

17

Than Sprowtok spak, 'Seis, sister, of your sorrow —
ye be too made for him sic murning mais.
We sall fair weill, I find Sanct Johne to borrow.
The proverb sayis as guid luif cumis as gais.
I will put on my hellye dayis clais,
and mak me fresch aganis this jolye May,
syne chant this sang, 'Was nevir wedow so gay'.

18

He was angrye and held us in grete aw,
and woundit with the speir of jelosye.
Off chaumer glew, Partlot, how weill ye knaw,
waistit he was, of nature cald and drye.
Sen he is gone, thairfore, sister, say I,
be blyith in bale for that is best remeid —
lat quik to quik and deid go to the deid.'

19

Thus Sprowtok spak that feynyeit faith befoir,
in luste but luif that sett all hir delyte,
'Sister, ye watte of sic as him a scoir
may it nocht siffise to slak your appetite.
I hecht you be my hand, sen ye ar quyte,
within a wolk — for schame and I durst speik —
to gett a berne could better claw your breik.'

20

Than Coppok like a curate spak full crous,
'Yone was ane verrye veangeance fra the hevin.
He was so loweous and so licherous,
seis coud he nocht with sissokkis mo than sevin.
Bot rychtuous God, haldand the ballaneis evin
smytis full soir, thocht he be patient,
adulteraris that list thame nocht repent.

21

Pridefull he was and joyit of his sin
and comptit nowther of Goddis falvour nor feid,
bot traistit ay to rax and sa furth rin,

till at the last his synnis could him leid
to schamefull end and to yone suddane deid.
Thairfore I wait it was the hand of God
that causit him be wirreit with the tod.'

22

Quhen this was said, the wedow fra hir swoun
stert up in haist and on hir kennattis cryid,
'How, Birkye, Burrye, Bell, Balsye broun,
Rypeschaw, Rynweill, Courtes, Cut and Clyid,
togidder all but gruncheing furth ye glyid.
Reskew my nobill cok or he be slane,
or ellis to me se ye cum nevir agane.'

23

With that but bade thay breddit our the bent
as fire of flint that our the feildis flaw,
wichtlye, I wis, throw woddis and watteris went
and swissit nocht ser Lourence till thay saw.
Bot quhen he saw the raches cum on raw,
unto the cok he said in mynde, 'God then
sen I and thou wer liftit in my den!'

24

Than spak the cok with sum guid spreit inspyrit,
'Do my counsale and I sall warrand thee.
Hungrie thou art and for grit travell tyrit,
rycht fant of force and may nocht forder flee.
Swyith turne agane and say that I and ye
freindis ar maid and fallowis for a yeir.
Than will thay stint, I stand for it, and nocht steir.'

25

This fox, thocht he was fals and frivelous
and hes fraudis his quarrellis to defend,
dissavit was throw mynis marvellous,
for falsheid failyeis at the latter end.
He turnit about and cryit as he was kend.
With that the cok brade out unto a buche.
Now reid ye sall quhairat ser Lourence luche.

26

Begylit thus, the tod under a tree
on knees fell and said, 'Gude Chanteclere,
cum doun agane and I but mete or fee
salbe your man and servand for ane yeir.'
'Nay, murther! theif and rivere, stand on reir!
My bludye hekkill and my nek so bla
hes pairtit love for evir betwene us twa.

27

I was unwyis that winkit at thy will
quhairthrow allmaist I lossit had my heid.'
'I was moir full,' quod he, 'could nocht be still,
bot spake to put my pray unto pleid.'
'Fair on, fals theif! God keip me fra thy feid!'
With that the cok our feildis tuke the flicht.
In at the wedowis lewar coud he licht.

28

Now, worthy folk, suppois this be a fable
and our helit with typis figurall,
yit may ye find a sentence rycht greabill

under the fenyeit termis textuall
Till oure purpois this cok wele may we call
a nice proud man void and vaneglorious,
off kin or gude quhilk is presumptuous.

29

Fy! pompous pryd, thou art rycht poysonable!
Quha favouris thee of force man have a fall.
Thy strength is nocht, thy stule standis unstable.
Tak witnes of the feindis infernall
quhilk huntit war doun fro the hevinly hall
to hellis hole and to that hidous hous
becaus of pride thay war presumptuous.

30

This feynit fox may wele be figurate
to flatteraris with plesand wirdis quhite,
with fals menyng and mouth mellifluate,
to loife and lee quhilk settis thair delyte.
All worthy folk at sic suld hafe dispyte,
for quhair is thair moir perilous pestilence
than giff to liaris haistelye credence?

31

This wikkit wind of adulatioun,
off swete socour haifand a similitude,
bittir as gall and full of fell poysoun
to taist it is, quha clerelye understude.
Forthy as now schortly for to conclude,
thir twa synnis, flattery and vaine glore,
ar venemous — guid folk, fle thame thairfore.

[63]

32

Leve we this wedow gled, I you assure,
off Chanteclere more blyith than I can tell,
and speke we of the fatal aventure
and destenye that to this fox befell
that durst no more with miching intermell
als lang as leme and lycht was of the day,
but bydand nycht full still lurkand he lay,

33

quhill that Thetes, the goddes of the flude,
Phebus had callit to the herverye,
and Esperus put of his cloudy hude,
schawand his lustye visage in the skye.
Than Lourence lukit up quhare he coud lye
and kest his hand upoun his ee on hicht,
mery and gled that cummyn was the nycht.

34

Out of the wod unto ane hill he went
quhare he mycht se the twinkling sternis clere
and all the planetis of the firmament,
thair coursis, and thair moving in thair sphere,
sum retrograde and sum war stationere,
and in the zodyak in quhit degree
thay were ilkane, as Lourance lerit me.

35

Than Saturne alde was enterit in Capricorne
and Jupiter movit in Sigittarye
and Mars up in the Rammys hede was borne

and Phebus in the Lyoun furth coud carye,
Venus the Crab, the Mone was in Aquarye,
Mercurius, the god of eloquence,
into the Virgin maid his residence.

36

Bot astrolab, quadrant or almanak,
techit of Nature be instructioun,
the moving of the hevin this tod can tak,
quhat influence and constillatioun
was lyk to fall upone this erd heir doun,
and to him self he said withouttin mair,
'Weill worth ye, fadir, that send me first to lair.

37

My destany and eik my werd I watt.
Myn evintour is cleirly to me kend.
With mischeif mynyet is my mortall fait
my mysleving the soner bot I mend.
Deid is reward of sin and schamefull end,
thairfoir I will ga seik sum confessour
and scryfe me clene of all synnis to this hour.

38

Allace!' quod he, 'rycht waryit ar we thevis!
Our life is sett ilk nycht in avinture.
Our cursit craft full mony ane mischevis,
for evir we steill and evir alyk ar pure.
In dreid and schame our dayis we indure
and widdy nek and crakraip callit als,
and syne till our hire ar hangit be the hals.

E

39

Accusand thus his cankerit conscience,
unto a craig he kest about his ee,
so saw he cumand a littill thane frome thence
a worthy Doctour of Divinite,
Freir Wolf Waitskath, in science wondrous sle,
to preche and pray was new cum of the clostir
with beidis in hand sayand his paternoster.

40

Seand the wolf, this wylie tratour tod
on kneis fell with hud in to his nek,
'Welcome, my gaistly fadir undir God'
quod he with mony binge and mony bek.
Than quod the wolf, 'Ser Fox, to what effek
mak ye sic feir? Rys up! Put on your hude!'
'Fader,' quod he, 'I haif grit caus to dude.

41

Ye ar the lanterne and the sicker way
suld gyd sic sympill folk as me to grace.
Your bair feit and your rousett coull of gray
schawis full weill your perfyt halynace,
your lene cheikis, your paill and petous face.
For weill war him that anis in his life
had hap to you his synnis anis to schryfe.'

42

'A, silly Lowrance,' quod the wolf and lewch,
'it plesis me that ye ar penitent.'
'Off reif and stowth, schir, I can tell ennewch

[66]

that causis me full sair for till repent.
Bot, fader, byd still heir on this bent,
I you beseik, and heir me now declair
my conscience that prikis me so sair.'

43

'Weill,' quod the wolf, 'sit doun upone thy kne',
and so he did bairheid full humly
and syn began with 'Benedicite'.
Quhen I thus saw I drew a littill by,
for it effeiris nowdir to heir nor spy
nor to reveill thing said undir that sele.
Than to the tod thus gait the wolf quod, 'Wele,

44

art thou contreit and sory in thy spreit
for thy trespas?' 'Nay, ser, I can nocht dude.
Me think that hennis ar swa hony sweit
and lambis flesch that new ar lattin blud,
for to repent my mind can nocht conclude
bot this thing — that I haif slane so few.'
'Weill,' quod the wolf, 'in south thou art a schrew.

45

Sen thou can nocht forthink thy wicketnais,
will thou forbeir in time cuming and mend?'
'And I forbeir, how sall I leif, allais!
haifand na uthir craft me to defend?
Neid causis me to steill quhairevir I wend.
I schame to thig. I can nocht wirk, ye wat.
yit wald I fane pretend a gentill stait.'

46

'Weill,' quod the wolf, 'thou wantis pontis twa
belangand to perfyt confessioun.
Now to the third pairte of pennance lat us ga.
Will thou tak pane for thy transgressioun?'
'A ser, considdir my complexioun,
and seikly and waik and of my natur tendir.
Lo, will ye se, I am baith lene and sklendir.

47

Yit nevir the les I wald, sa it wer lycht
and schort, nocht grevand to my tendirnes,
tak pairte of pane, fulfill it gife I micht,
to sett my silly saule in way of grace.'
'Thou sall forbeir,' quod he, 'flesche hyne to Pais
to tame thy cors, that cursit carioun,
and heir I reik thee full remissioun.'

48

'I grant thairto, sa ye will gife me leif
to eit puddingis or laip a littill blude,
or heid and feit or penchis lat me preif
in cais I fant of flesche in to my fude.'
'For grit mister I gife thee leif to dude
twys in the owlk, for neid may haif no law.'
'God yeild you, ser, for that text full weill ye knaw.'

49

Quhen this was said, the wolf his wayis went.
The fox on fute he fure unto the flude.
To fang sum fische wes hellely his intent,

bot quhen he saw thir walterand wavis wude,
all stoneist still into a stair he stude
and said, 'Bettir that I had biddin at hame
than be a fischar, in the devillis name!

50

Now mon I skraip my meit out of the sand,
for I haif nowdir net, bottis nor bate.'
As he wes thus for falt of meit murnand,
lukand about his leving for to late,
undir a tre he saw a trip of gate.
Than wes he fane and in a huche him hid
and fra the gait he stall a littill kid.

51

Syne our the huche unto the se him hyis
and tuk the kid rycht be the hornis twane
and in the wattir owther twys or thrys
he dowkit him and thus gait cowth he sane,
'Ga doun ser kid, cum up ser salmound agane,'
quhill he wes deid, syne to the land him drewch
and of that new made salmond eit ennewch.

52

Thus fynaly fillit with tendir meit
unto a den for dreid he hes him drest.
Undir a busk quhair that the sone cowth beit
to beke his breist and bellye he thocht best
and rakleslye he said quhair he coud rest,
strakand his wambe agane this sonnes hete,
'Upoun this bellye ware sett a bolt full mete.'

53

Quhen this was said, the kepare of the gayte,
carefull in hert his kid was stollin away,
on everye side full warlye culd he wayte
till at the last he saw quhair Lowrence lay.
His bow he bent. A flane with fedderis gray
he hailit to the heid. Or evir he sterd,
the fox fast he prikkit to the erd.

54

'Now,' quod the fox, 'alace and welloway,
gorrit I am and may no forther gane.
Me think no man may speke a word in play
bot now on dayis in ernist it is tane.'
The hird him hynt and out he drew his flane
and for his kid and uther violence
he tuke his skin and maid a recompence.

55

This suddane deid and unprovisit end
off this fals tod without contritioun
exemple is exhortand folk to mend
for dreid of sic a like conclusioun.
For monye gois now to confessioun
can nocht repent nor for thair synnis greit
becaus thai think thair lustye life so sweit.

56

Sum bene also throw consuetude and ryte
vincust with carnall sensualitie.
Suppose thay be as for the time contrite,

can nane forbere nor fra thair synnis flee.
Use drawis nature so in propertie
off beist and man that nedis thay mon do
as thay of lang time thame have hantit to.

57

Beware, guid folk, and dreid this suddane schote
quhilk smytis soir withouttin resistence.
Attent wyislye and in your hartis note
aganis deid may no man mak defence.
Ceis of your sin. Remord your conscience.
Do wilfull pennance here and ye sall wend
eftir your deid to joy withouttin end.

58

This foirsaid fox thus deid for his misdede
had nocht a sone was gottin rychtuuslye
that to his airschip mycht of law succede
except ane sone, the quhilk in lemanrye
he gottin had in purchase prively
and to his name was clepit Fader wer,
that lufit wele with pultry tig and tere.

59

It followis wele be reasoun naturale
and gree by gree of rycht comparisoun,
off evill cumis war, of ware cummys warst of all,
off wrangus get cummys wrang successioun.
This fox, bastard of generatioun,
off verrye kind behufit to be fals —
so was his grantser and his fader als.

60

As Nature will, sekand his fude be sent,
off cais he fand his faderis caryon,
naikit, new slane, and till him is he went,
tuke up his hede, syne on his kneis fel doun,
thankand grete God of that conclusioun
and said, 'Now sall I brouk, sen I am aire,
the boundis quhare he wont was to repaire.'

61

Fy! covetous unkind and venemous.
The sone was fain he fand his fader dede
be sudane schote for dedeis odious
that he mycht rax and regne into his stede,
dredand nothing that samin lyife to lede
in stouth and reif as he had done before,
bot to the end entent he tuke no more.

62

Yit nevirtheles for faderlye pitee
the caryon upoun his bak he tais.
'Now find I wele this proverbe trew,' quod he,
'Ay rynnis the fox als lang as he fut hais.'
Syne with his cors unto a petpot gais
off watere full and kest him in the depe
and to the devill his banis gave to kepe.

63

O fulich man, ploungit in wardlynes,
to conquest wrangwis guidis, gold or rent,
to put thy saule in pane and hevynes

to riche thine air, quhilk efter thou be went,
have he thy gude, he takis small entent
to sing or say for thy salvatioun!
Fra thou be dede, done is devotioun.

64

This tod to rest he carit to a crag
and herd a bustous bugill brymly blawe
quhilk, as him thocht, maid all this warld to wag.
Than stert I up and cumand nere I sawe
ane unicorne semely lansand our ane lawe
with horne in hand; ane buste on brest he bure,
a pursevant semely, I you assure.

65

Unto a bank quhair he mycht se about
on everye side in haste he coud him hye,
put furth his voce full loud and gave a schout
and 'Oyas, oyas' twis or thris coud cry.
With that the bestis in the feildis nere by,
all mervailand quhat sic a cry suld mene,
govand agast, thai gadderit on a grene.

66

Out of his buste a bill sone coud he braide
and red the text withouttyn tarying.
Commaundand silence, sadly thus he said,
'We, Nobill Lyoun, of all beistis king,
greting in God ay lestand but ending
to brutall bestis and irrationall
I send as to my subjectis grete and small.

67

My celsitude and hie magnificence,
lattis you wit furthwith incontinent,
thinkis to morne with riall diligence
upoun this hill to hald a parliament.
Straitlye thairfore I geve commandiment
for to compeir before my tribunall,
under all pane and parrell that may fall.'

68

The morowing come and Phebus with his bemys
consumit had the misty cloudis gray.
The ground was grene and as the gold it glemys
with gresis growand gudelie grete and gay.
The spice than spred to spring on every spray.
The lark, the mavis and the merle so hee
swetlye can sing, trippand fra tree to tree.

69

Thre leopardis come. A croun of massy gold
berand thay brocht unto that hillis hicht,
with jaspis junyt and riall rubies rold
and monye divers dyamantis wele dicht.
With pollis proud a palyoun doun thay picht
and in that trone thair sat a wild lyoun
in rob riale with ceptur, swerd and croun.

70

Efter the tennour of the crye before
thair gais on fut all bestis in the erd.
Rycht as thay ware commandit without more

before thair lord the lion thay comperd
and quhat thay ware, as tod Lourence me lerd,
I sall rehers a pairt of every kind,
als far as now occurris to my mind.

71

The Menataur, a monstour mervelous,
Bellerophant, that beist of bastarde,
the warwolf and the Pegas perolus
transformit be assent of socerre,
the lynx, the tegir full of tyrrane,
the oliphant and eik the dromodare;
the camell with his cran craig furth culd care.

72

The leopard, as I haif taute beforne,
the antelop; the sparth furth culd hir speid,
the paynttit panther and the unicorne;
the raynder ran throuch rever, ron and reid;
the jolye jonet and the gentill steid,
the aiss, the mul, the hors of everye kind,
the de, the re, the hornit hairt, the hind.

73

The bull, the beir, the bugill and the bair,
the wodwys, wildcat and the wild wolfyne,
the hard bak hurtchoun and the hyrpilland hair,
bayth ottour, aip and pennytt porcapyne,
the guckit gait, the wyllye scheip, the swyne,
the baver, bakon and the batterand brok,
the fumard with the fyber furth culd flok.

74

The gay gruhund, the sleuthhund furth can slyd
with doggis all dyvers and deferent.
The rattoun ran, the globert furth culd glyd,
the quherland quhithrat with the wasyll wentt,
the fythow that hes furrit mony ane fent,
the martryk with the cunyng and the con,
the lurdane lane and eik the lerrion.

75

The mermissat the modewart could leid
becaus that natour denyit had hir sycht.
Thus dressit thay all furth for dreid of deid.
The musk, the litill mows with all hir mycht
in haist haykit unto that hillis hycht
and mony ane kind of beist that I nocht knaw
befoir thair lord ilkane thay lowtit law.

76

Seand thir beistis at his bidding bown,
he gave a braide and blenkit all about.
Than flatlingis to his feit thay fell all doun.
For dreid of deid thay drowpit all in dout.
The lyoun lukit quhen he saw thame lout
and bad thaim with ane countenance full sweit,
'Be nocht afferit bot stand upoun your feit.

77

I lat you wit my mycht is merceabill
and steris none that ar to me prostrat,
angrye, austerne and als unameabill

to all that standfray ar to mine estait.
I rug, I rive all beistis that makis debait.
Aganis the mycht of my magnefecence
se none pretend to pride in my presence.

78

My celsitude and my hie majestye
with mycht and mercye myngit salbe ay.
The lawest heir I may rycht sone up hie
and mak him maister ouer you all I may.
The dromadair gif he will mak deray,
or the greit cameill, thocht thay be never sa crous,
I can thame law as litill as ane mous.

79

Se neir be twenty mylis quhair I am
the kid ga salflie be the wolfis side.
Se tod Lowrye luke nocht upoun the lamb,
na revand beistis nowther ryn nor ride.'
Thay cucheit all and efter this wes cryit,
the justice bad anone the court do fens,
the sutis call and foirfalt all absens.

80

The panthere with his payntit coit armour
fensit the court as he of law effeirit.
Tod Laurence lukit up quhair he could lour
and stert on fute all stoneist and all sterit.
Ryvand his hair he rarit with a reird,
quakand for dreid ran, sichand could he say,
'Allace! this hour, allace! this wofull day.

81

I wait this suddane semblay that I se,
havand the poyntis of a parliament,
is maid to mar sic misdoaris as me.
Thairfoir, and I me schaw, I wilbe schent.
I wilbe socht gif I be red absent —
to bide or fle it makis no remeid,
all is alike, thair followis nocht bot deid.'

82

Perplexit thus in to his mind can mene
with falsheid quhow he mycht him self defend.
His hude he drew far doun attour his ene
and wynkand with the ane ee furth can wend.
Clyncheand he come that he suld nocht be kend
and for dreddour that he suld thoill areist
he playit bukhud anone fra beist to beist.

83

Compering thus he come befoir the king.
In ordour sett as to thair stait efferit,
off everye kind he gart ane pairt furth bring
and awfulye he spak and at thame speirit
gif thair wis ony beist in to this erd
absent, and thair gart thaim all deiplie swere
and thay said nay, except ane gray stude meir.

84

'Go mak ane message sone unto that stude.'
The court than cryit, 'My lord, quha sall that be?'
'Cum heir, Lowrie, lurkand undir ane hude.'

'A lord, mercye! Lo, I have bot ane ee,
hurt in the hanch and crukit ye may se.
The wolf is bettir in ambassadry
and mair cunning in clergye fer than I.'

85

Braiding he said, 'Go furth, ye brybouris bayth',
and thay to ga withoutin tareying
our ron and riyce thay ran togidder rayth
and fand the meir at meit in the morning.
'How,' quod the tod, 'madame, go to the king.
The court is callit and ye ar *contumax*.'
'Lat be, Laurence, your carping and your knax.'

86

'Maistres,' quod he, 'cum to the court ye mon.
The lyoun hes commandit you in deid.'
'Laurence, tak you the flirdome and the fon,
I have a respit heir and ye will rede.'
'I can nocht spell a word, sa God me speid.
Heir is the wolf, a nobill clerk at all
and of this message he is principall.

87

He is autentik and a man of aige
and hes the practik of the chancellary.
Lat him ga luke and reid your previlege
and I sall stand and beir you witnes by.'
'Quhair is your respit?' quod the wolf in hy.
'Sir, it is heir under my hoise weill hid.'
'Hald up your hele,' quod he, and sa scho did.

88

Thocht he wes brynt throuch pride, yit he presumis
to luke doun law quhair that thir lettres lay.
With that the mere scho gird him on the gumys
and strake the hattrell of his hede away.
Half out of life lenand doun he lay.
'Alace,' quod Lourence, 'Lupus, that thou art lost!'
'His conyng', quod the mere, 'was wirth sum cost.

89

Lourans, will thou nocht luke upoun my letter
sen that the wolf thairof can nothing win?'
'Nay, be Sanct Bryde,' quod he, 'me think far better
to slepe in hele and in ane unhurt skin.
A scrow I fand and thus writtin thairin —
for five schillingis I wald nocht anys faltum —
felix quem faciunt aliena pericula cautum.'

90

With brokin scalp and bludye chekis rede
this wolf wepand on his way is went.
Off his maynye merkand to gete remede
to tell the king the cais was his entent.
'Schir,' quod the tod, 'bid still upoun the bent
and fra your browis wesche away the blude
and tak a drink, for it will do you gude.'

91

To fech water this fraudfull fox furth fure.
Sidlingis a bank he socht unto a sike.
Off cais he metis cumand fra the mure

[80]

a trip of lambis dansand on a dike.
This traytour tod, this tyran and this tike
the fattest of the flok he fellit has
and ete his fill, syne to the wolf he gais.

92

Thay drank but tary and thair journay takis,
befoir the king syne knelit on thare knee.
'Quhare is the mere, ser tod, was *contumax*?'
Than Lourance said, 'My lord, spere nocht at me.
This new maid Doctour of Divinitee
with his rede cap can tell you wele yneuch.'
With that, the lion and the lave thay leuch.

93

'Tell on the cais, ser Lourence, lat us here.'
'This witty wolf, this noble clerk of aige,
on your behalf he bad the mere compere
and scho allegit till a previlege —
'Cum nere and se and ye sall have your wage.'
Becaus he red hir respit plane and wele,
yone rede bannete scho raucht him with hir hele.'

94

The lion said, 'Be yone rede cap I ken
this tale is trew, quha tent unto it takis,
'the grettest clerkis ar nocht the wisest men.
a mannis hurt ane other happy makis.' "
As thay ware carpand thusgatis in knakis
and all the court in garray and in gam,
sa come the yow, the moder of the lam.

95

Before the justice doun on knees fell,
put furth hir plaint on this wis wofullye,
'This harlot here, this hursoun hund of hell,
he werryit hes my lam full doggitlye
within a mile incontrare of your cry.
For Goddis lufe, my lord, gif me the lawe
off this lymmar!' With that Lourence lete drawe.

96

'Bide!' quod the lion. 'Lemmar, lat us se
giff this be suyth the sely yow has said.'
'A soverane lord, sauf your mercy,' quod he,
'my purpois was with him bot to have plaid.
Causles he fell as he had bene affraid.
For drede of deid he duschit our a dike
and brak his nek.' 'Thou leis,' quod scho, 'fals tike.

97

His dede be practik may be previt eth —
thy gorry gomys and thy bludy snout,
the woll, the flesche yit stikkis in thy teth
and that is evident eneuch but dout.'
The justice bad go cheis asis about
and so thay did and fand that he was fals
off murthour, thift and party treson als.

98

Thay band him fast. The justice bad belyve
to geve the dome and tak of all his clathis.
The wolf, that new maid doctour, coud him schryve,

syne furth with him unto the gallowis gais
and at the ledder fute his leve he tais.
The ape was basare and bad him sone ascend
and hangit him and thus he maid ane end.

99

Rycht as the mynoure in his mynorall
faire gold with fire may fra the lede wele win,
rycht sa under a fable figurall
a sad sentence may seke and efter fyn,
as daylie dois thir doctouris of dyvyn,
apertly be our leving can applye
and preve thare preching be a poesye.

100

The lion is this warld be liklynace
to quhom lowtis bayth emperour and king
and thinkis of this warld to get mare grace
and gapis for to get thame mare lifing,
sum for to reule and sum to rax and regne.
Sum gadderis gere, sum gold, sum uther gude.
To win this warld sum wirkis as thay wer wode.

101

This mere is men of contemplatioun,
off pennance walkand in this wildernace,
as monkis and othir men of religioun
that presis God to pleis in every place,
abstrackit fra this warldis wretchidnes,
in wilfull povertee fra pomp and pride,
and fra this warld in mind ar mortifyde.

102

This wolf I likkin unto sensualitee,
as quhen like brutall bestis we accord
our mind all to this warldeis vanitee,
liking to tak and love him as our lord.
Fle fast thairfra gif thou will rycht remord.
Than sall Reasoun ris, rax and ring
and for thy saull thair is no better thing.

103

Hir hufe I likkin to the thocht of dede.
Will thou remembere, man, that thou man dee,
thow may brek sensualiteis hede
and fleschlye lust away fra thee sall flee.
Wis Salomon sais, will thou nocht see?
For as thou may thy sely saull now win
think on thine end, thou sall nocht gladlye sin.

104

This tod I likin to temptatioun,
berand to mind monye thochtis vane,
that daylie sagis men of religioun,
cryand to thame, 'Cum to the warld agane.'
Bot quhen thay see sensualitie neir slane
and sudane dede with ithand panis sore,
he gois abak and tempis thame no more.

105

O Mary mild, medeator of mercy meke,
sitt doun before thy Sone celestiall,
for us synnaris his celsitude beseke

ROBERT HENRYSON

us to defend fra payne and perallis all
and help us up unto that hevinlye hall
in glore quhair we may see the sycht of God.
And thus endis the talking of the tod.

ANONYMOUS

IV

From *The Taill of Rauf Coilyear how he harbreit King Charlis*

1

In the cheiftime of Charlis that chosin chiftane
thair fell ane ferlyfull flan within thay fellis wide
quhair empreouris and erlis and uther mony ane
turnit fra Sanct Thomas befoir the Yule tide.
Thay past unto Paris, thay proudest in pane,
with mony prelatis and princis that was of mekle pride.
All thay went with the King to his worthy wane,
ouir the feildis sa fair thay fure be his side.
All the worthiest went in the morning,
    baith dukis and duchepeiris,
    barrounis and bacheleiris.
  Mony stout man steiris
    of toun with the King

2

And as that ryall raid ouir the rude mure,
him betide ane tempest that time hard I tell.
The wind blew out of the eist stiflie and sture,
the drift durandlie draif in mony deip dell.

Sa feirslie fra the firmament, sa fellounlie it fure
thair micht na folk hald na fure on the heich fell.
In point thay war to parische thay proudest men and pure,
in thay wickit wedderis thair wist nane to dwell.
Amang thay mirk montanis sa madlie thay mer,
      be it was prime of the day
      sa wonder hard fure thay
      that ilk ane tuik ane seir way
        and sperpellit full fer.

3

Ithand wedderis of the eist draif on sa fast
it all to blaisterit and blew that thairin baid.
Be thay disseverit sindrie midmorne was past.
Thair wist na knicht of the Court quhat way the King
    raid.
He saw thair was na better bot God at the last.
His steid aganis the storme stalwartlie straid.
He cachit fra the Court, sic was his awin cast,
quhair na body was him about be five mylis braid.
In thay montanis, I wis, he wox all will
      in wickit wedderis and wicht
      amang thay montanis on hicht.
      Be that it drew to the nicht
        the King lykit ill.

4

Evill lykand was the King it nichtit him sa lait
and he na harberie had for his behufe.

ANONYMOUS

Sa come thair ane cant Carll cachand the gait
with ane capill and twa creillis cuplit abufe.
The King carpit to the Carll withoutin debait,
'Schir, tell me thy richt name for the Rude lufe.'
He sayis, 'Menn callis me Rauf Coilyear, as I weill
    wait.
I leid my life in this land with mekle unrufe
baith tide and time in all my travale.
        Hine ouir sevin mylis I dwell
        and leidis coilis to sell.
        Sen thou speiris, I thee tell
           all the suith hale.

5

'Sa mot I thrife.' said the King, 'I speir for nane ill.
Thou semis ane nobill fallow, thy answer is sa fine.'
'Forsuith,' said the Coilyear, 'traist quhen thou will,
for I trow, and it be nocht swa, sumpart salbe thine.'
'Mary, God forbid,' said the King, 'that war bot lytill
    skill.
Baith my self and my hors is reddy for to tyne.
I pray thee, bring me to sum rest, the wedder is sa
    schill,
for I defend that we fall in ony fechtine —
I had mekill mair nait sum freindschip to find
        and gif thou can better than I,
        for the name of Sanct July,
        thou bring me to sum harbery
          and leif me not behind.'

ANONYMOUS

6

'I wait na worthie harberie heir neir hand
for to serve sic ane man as me think thee,
nane bot mine awin hous maist in this land
fer furth in the Forest amang the fellis hie.
With thy thou wald be payit of sic as thou fand,
forsuith thou suld be welcum to pas hame with me,
or ony uther gude fallow that I heir fand
walkand will of his way, as me think thee,
for the wedderis ar sa fell that fallis on the feild.'
　　　　The King was blyth quhair he raid
　　　　　　of the grant he had maid,
　　　　　　sayand with hart glaid,
　　　　　　　　'Schir, God you foryeild!'

7

'Na, thank me not ouir airlie for dreid that we threip,
for I have servit thee yit of lytill thing to ruse,
for nouther hes thou had of me fire, drink nor meit,
nor nane uther eismentis for travellouris behufe,
bot micht we bring this harberie this nicht weill to heip
that we micht with ressoun baith thus excuse,
tomorne, on the morning quhen thou fall on leip,
prys at the parting how that thou dois,
for first to lose and syne to lak, Peter, it is schame!'
　　　　The King said, 'In gude fay,
　　　　　　schir, it is suith that ye say.'
　　　　Into sic talk fell thay
　　　　　　quhill thay war neir hame.

8

To the Coilyearis hous, baith or thay wald blin,
the Carll had cunning weill quhair the gait lay.
'Undo the dure belive! Dame, art thou in?
Quhy devill makis thou na dule for this evill day?
For my gaist and I baith cheveris with the chin.
Sa fell ane wedder feld I never, be my gude fay!'
The gude wife glaid with the gle to begin,
for durst scho never sit summoundis that scho hard him
    say.
The Carll was wantoun of word and wox wonder
    wraith.
        All abaisit for blame
        to the dure went our dame.
        Scho said, 'Schir, ye ar welcome hame
          and your gaist baith.'

9

'Dame, I have deir coft all this dayis hire,
in wickit wedderis and weit walkand full will.
Dame, kyith I am cummin hame and kendill on ane
    fire.
I trow our gaist be the gait hes farne als ill.
Ane ryall rufe het fire war my desire.
To fair the better, for his saik gif we micht win thair
    till,
knap doun capounis of the best but in the byre.
Heir is bot hamelie fair! Do belive, Gill!'

Twa cant knaifis of his awin haistelie he bad,
    'The ane of you my capill ta,
    the uther his coursour alswa.
    To the stabill swyith ye ga!'
    Than was the King glaid.

10

The Coilyear gudlie in feir tuke him be the hand
and put him befoir him as ressoun had bene.
Quhen thay come to the dure the King begouth to
    stand,
to put the Coilyear in befoir maid him to mene.
He said, 'Thou art uncourtes, that sall I warrand.'
He tyt the King be the nek twa part in tene.
'Gif thou at bidding suld be boun or obeysand
and gif thou of courtasie couth, thou hes foryet it clene.
Now is anis,' said the Coilyear, 'kind aucht to creip,
    sen ellis thou art unknawin,
    to mak me lord of my awin.
    Sa mot I thrive, I am thrawin,
    begin we to threip!'

11

Than benwart thay yeid quhair brandis was bricht
to ane bricht byrnand fire as the Carll bad.
He callit on Gyliane his wife thair supper to dicht,
'Of the best that thair is, help that we had
efter ane evill day to have ane mirrie nicht,
for sa troublit with stormis was I never stad,

[91]

of ilk airt of the eist sa laithly it laid.
    Yit was I mekle willar than
    quhen I met with this man.'
    Of sic taillis thay began
      quhill the supper was graid.

12

Sone was the supper dicht and the fire bet
and thay had weschin, I wis, the worthiest was thair,
'Tak my wife be the hand in feir withoutin let
and gang begin the buird,' said the Coilyear.
'That war unsemand forsuith and thy self unset.'
The King profferit him to gang and maid ane strange
    fair,
'Now is twyse,' said the Carl, 'me think thou hes
    foryet.'
He leit gird to the King withoutin ony mair
and hit him under the eir with his richt hand
    quhill he stakkerit thair with all
    half the breid of the hall.
    He faind never of ane fall
      quhill he the eird fand.

13

He start up stoutly agane — uneis micht he stand
for anger of that outray that he had thair tane.
He callit on Gyliane his wife, 'Ga, tak him be the hand
and gang agane to the buird quhair ye suld air have
    gane.

Schir, thou art unskilfull and that sall I warrand.
Thou byrd to have nurtour aneuch and thou hes nane.
Thou hes walkit, I wis, in mony wild land.
The mair vertew thou suld have to keip thee fra blame.
Thou suld be courtes of kind and ane cunnand courteir.
> Thocht that I simpill be,
> do as I bid thee.
> The hous is mine, pardie,
> and all that is heir.'

14

The King said to him self, 'This is ane evill life.
Yit was I never in my life thus gait leird
and I have oft times bene quhair gude hes bene rife
that maist couth of courtasie in this Cristin eird.
Is nane sa gude as leif of and mak na mair strife,
for I am stonischit at this straik that hes me thus steird.'
In feir fairlie he foundis with the gude wife,
quhair the Coilyear bad sa braithlie he beird.
Quhen he had done his bidding as him gude thocht,
> doun he sat the King neir
> and maid him glaid and gude cheir
> and said, 'Ye ar welcum heir,
> be him that me bocht.'

15

Quhen thay war servit and set to the suppar,
Gyll and the gentill King Charlis of micht,
syne on the tother side sat the Coilyear;
thus war thay marschellit but mair and matchit that nicht.

Thay brocht breid to the buird and brawn of ane bair
and the worthiest wine went upon hicht.
Thay beirnis, as I wene, thay had aneuch thair
within that burelie bigging byrnand full bricht.
Syne enteris thair daynteis, on deis dicht dayntelie
within that worthie wane.
Forsuith wantit thay nane.
With blyith cheir sayis Gyliane,
'Schir, dois gladlie.'

16

The Carll carpit to the King cumlie and cleir,
'Schir, the Forestaris forsuith of this Forest
thay have me all at invy for dreid of the deir.
Thay threip that I thring doun of the fattest.
Thay say I sall to Paris thair to compeir
befoir our cumlie King in dule to be drest.
Sic manassing thay me mak forsuith ilk yeir
and yit aneuch sall I have for me and ane gest.
Thairfoir sic as thou seis, spend on and not spair.
Thus said gentill Charlis the Mane
to the Coilyear agane,
'The King him self hes bene fane
sum time of sic fair.'

17

Of capounis and cunningis thay had plentie,
with wine at thair will and eik vennysoun,
byrdis bakin in breid, the best that may be.
Thus full freschlie thay fure into fusioun.

The Carll with ane cleir voce carpit on he,
said, 'Gyll, lat the cop raik for my bennysoun
and gar our gaist begin and syne drink thou to me;
sen he is ane stranger, me think it ressoun.'
Thay drank dreichlie about, thay wosche and thay rais.
> The King with ane blyith cheir
> thankit the Coilyeir,
> syne all the thre into feir
> to the fire gais.

18

Quhen thay had maid thame eis, the Coilyear tald
mony sindrie taillis efter suppair.
Ane bricht byrnand fire was byrnand full bald.
The King held gude countenance and company bair
and ever to his asking ane answer he yald
quhill at the last he began to frane farther mair.
'In faith, freind, I wald wit, tell gif ye wald,
quhair is thy maist wynning?' said the Coilyear.
'Out of weir,' said the King, 'I wayndit never to tell.
> With my lady the Quene
> in office maist have I bene
> all thir yeiris fyftene
> in the Court for to dwell.'

19

'Quhat kin office art thou in quhen thou art at hame,
gif thou dwellis with the Quene, proudest in pane?'
'Ane Child of hir Chalmer, schir, be Sanct Jame,
and thocht my self it say, maist inwart of ane.

For my dwelling to nicht I dreid me for blame.'
'Quhat sal I cal thee,' said the Coilyear, 'quhen thou
    art hyne gane?'
'Wymond of the Wardrop is my richt name.
Quhair ever thou findis me befoir thee, thy harberie is
    tane.
And thou will cum to the Court, this I underta,
       thou sall have for thy fewaill
       for my saik the better saill
       and onwart to thy travaill
         worth ane laid or twa.'

20

He said, 'I have na knawledge quhair the Court lyis
and I am wunder wa to cum quhair I am unkend.'
'And I sall say thee the suith on ilk side, I wis
that thou sall wit weill aneuch or I fra thee wend.
Baith the King and the Quene meitis in Paris
for to hald thair Yule togidder, for scho is efter send.
Thair may thou sell be ressoun als deir as thou will
    prys,
and yit I sall help thee, gif I ocht may amend,
for I am knawin with officiaris in cais thou cum
    thair.
       Have gude thocht on my name
       and speir gif I be at hame,
       for I suppois be Sanct Jame
        thou sall the better fair.'

21

'Me think it ressoun, be the Rude, that I do thy red,
in cais I cum to the Court and knaw bot thee ane.
Is nane sa gude as drink and gang to our bed,
for, als far as I wait, the nicht is furth gane.'
To ane previe chalmer belive thay him led
quhair ane burely bed was wrocht in that wane
closit with courtingis and cumlie cled.
Of the worthiest wine wantit thay nane.
The Coilyear and his wife baith with him thay yeid
      to serve him all at thay mocht
        till he was in bed brocht.
      Mair the King spak nocht
        bot thankit thame thair deid.

V

Jerusalem rejos for joy:
Jesus, the sterne of most bewte
in thee is rissin as richtous roy,
fro dirknes to illumyne thee.
With glorius sound of angell gle
thy prince is borne in Baithlem
quhilk sall thee mak of thraldome fre.
Illuminare Jerusalem.

With angellis licht in legionis
thou art illumynit all about.
Thre kingis of strenge regionis
to thee ar cumin with lusty rout,

all drest with dyamantis but dout,
reverst with gold in every hem,
sounding attonis with a schout,
Illuminare Jerusalem.

The regeand tirrant that in thee rang,
Herod, is exilit and his ofspring,
The land of Juda that josit wrang,
and rissin is now thy richtous king.
So he so mychtie is and ding,
quhen men his glorius name dois nem,
hevin erd and hell makis inclyning.
Illuminare Jerusalem.

His cummyng knew all element —
the air be sterne did him persaife:
the watter quhen dry he on it went:
the erd that trymlit all and raife:
the sone quhen he no lichtis gaif:
the croce quhen it wes done contem:
the stanis quhen thay in pecis claif:
Illuminare Jerusalem.

The deid him knew that rais upricht
quhilk lang time had the erd lyne undir:
crukit and blind declarit his micht
that helit of thame so mony hundir:
Nature him knew and had grit wundir
quhen he of virgin wes borne but wem:
Hell, quhen thair yettis were brokin asundir.
Illuminare Jerusalem.

[98]

WILLIAM DUNBAR
(c. 1460–c. 1513)

VI

On his Heid-ake

My heid did yak yester nicht,
this day to mak that I na micht,
  so sair the magryme dois me menyie,
  perseing my brow as ony ganyie,
that scant I luik may on the licht.

And now, schir, laitlie, eftir mes,
to dyt thocht I begowthe to dres,
  the sentence lay full evill till find,
  unsleipit in my heid behind,
dullit in dulnes and distres.

Full oft at morrow I upryse,
quhen that my curage sleipeing lyis,
  for mirth, for menstrallie and play,
  for din nor danceing nor deray,
it will nocht walkin me no wise.

WILLIAM DUNBAR

VII

Meditatioun in Wyntir

In to thir dirk and drublie dayis,
quhone sabill all the hevin arrayis
  with mystie vapouris, cluddis, and skyis,
  Nature all curage me denyis
off sangis, ballattis, and of playis.

Quhone that the nycht dois lenthin houris,
with wind, with haill, and havy schouris,
  my dule spreit dois lurk for schoir,
  my hairt for languor dois forloir
for laik of symmer with his flouris.

I walk, I turne, sleip may I nocht,
I vexit am with havie thocht;
  this warld all ouir I cast about,
  and ay the mair I am in dout,
the mair that I remeid have socht.

I am assayit on everie syde:
Dispair sayis ay, 'In tyme provyde
  and get sum thing quhairon to leif,
  or with grit trouble and mischeif
thow sall in to this court abyd.'

WILLIAM DUNBAR

Than Patience sayis, 'Be not agast:
hald Hoip and Treuthe within the fast,
  and lat Fortoun wirk furthe hir rage,
  quhome that no rasoun may assuage,
quhill that hir glas be run and past.'

And Prudence in my eir sayis ay,
'Quhy wald thow hald that will away?
  or craif that thow may have no space,
  thow tending to ane uther place,
a journay going everie day?'

And than sayis Age, 'My freind, cum neir,
and be not strange, I the requeir:
  cum, brodir, by the hand me tak,
  Remember thow hes compt to mak
off all thi tyme thow spendit heir.'

Syne Deid castis upe his yettis wyd,
saying, 'Thir oppin sall the abyd;
  albeid that thow wer never sa stout,
  undir this lyntall sall thow lowt:
thair is nane uther way besyde.

For feir of this all day I drowp;
no gold in kist, nor wyne in cowp,
  no ladeis bewtie, nor luiffis blys,
  may lat me to remember this,
how glaid that ever I dyne or sowp.

Yit, quhone the nycht begynnis to schort,
it dois my spreit sum pairt confort,
   off thocht oppressit with the schowris.
   Cum, lustie symmer! with thi flowris,
that I may leif in sum disport.

VIII

To a Ladye

Sweit rois of vertew and of gentilnes,
delytsum lyllie of everie lustynes,
   richest in bontie and in bewtie cleir,
   and everie vertew that is held most deir,
except onlie that ye ar mercyles.

In to your garthe this day I did persew,
thair saw I flowris that fresche wer of hew;
   baith quhyte and reid moist lusty wer to seyne,
   and halsum herbis upone stalkis grene;
yit leif nor flour fynd could I nane of rew.

I dout that Merche, with his caild blastis keyne,
hes slane this gentill herbe that I of mene,
   quhois petewous deithe dois to my hart sic pane
   that I wald mak to plant his rute agane,
so confortand his levis unto me bene.

IX

To the Merchantis of Edinburgh

Quhy will ye, merchantis of renoun,
lat Edinburgh, your nobill toun,
for laik of reformatioun
the commone proffeitt tyine and fame?
   Think ye not schame,
that onie uther regioun
sall with dishonour hurt your name!

May nane pas throw your principall gaittis
for stink of haddockis and of scattis,
for cryis of carlingis and debaittis,
for fensum flyttingis of defame.
   Think ye not schame,
befoir strangeris of all estaittis
that sic dishonour hurt your name!

Your stinkand Scull, that standis dirk,
haldis the lycht fra your parroche kirk;
your foirstairis makis your housis mirk,
lyk na cuntray bot heir at hame.
   Think ye not schame,
sa litill polesie to wirk
in hurt and sclander of your name!

At your hie Croce, quhar gold and silk
sould be, thair is bot crudis and milk;
and at your Trone bot cokill and wilk,
pansches, pudingis of Jok and Jame.
    Think ye not schame,
sen as the world sayis that ilk
in hurt and sclander of your name!

Your commone menstrallis hes no tone
bot 'Now the day dawis,' and 'Into Joun';
cunningar men man serve Sanct Cloun,
and nevir to uther craftis clame.
    Think ye not schame,
to hald sic mowaris on the moyne,
in hurt and sclander of your name!

Tailyouris, soutteris, and craftis vyll,
the fairest of your streitis dois fyll;
and merchandis at the Stinkand Styll
ar hamperit in ane hony came.
    Think ye not schame,
that ye have nether witt nor wyll
to win yourselff ane bettir name!

Your burgh of beggeris is ane nest,
to schout thai swentyouris will not rest;
all honest folk they do molest,
sa piteuslie thai cry and rame.
    Think ye not schame,
that for the poore hes nothing drest,
in hurt and sclander of your name!

[104]

WILLIAM DUNBAR

Your proffeit daylie dois incres,
your godlie workis les and les;
through streittis nane may mak progres
for cry of cruikit, blind, and lame.
   Think ye not schame,
that ye sic substance dois posses,
and will nocht win ane bettir name!

Sen for the Court and the Sessioun,
the great repair of this regioun
is in your burgh, thairfoir be boun
to mend all faultis that ar to blame,
   and eschew schame;
gif thai pas to ane uther toun
ye will decay, and your great name!

Thairfoir strangeris and leigis treit,
tak not ouer meikle for thair meit,
and gar your merchandis be discreit,
that na extortiounes be, proclame
   all fraud and schame:
keip ordour, and poore nighbouris beit,
that ye may gett ane bettir name!

Singular proffeit so dois yow blind,
the common proffeit gois behind:
I pray that Lord remeid to fynd,
that deit into Jerusalem.
   and gar yow schame!
that sum tyme ressoun may yow bind,
for to [   ] yow guid name.

X

Epetaphe for Donald Owre

In vice most vicius he excellis,
that with the vice of tressone mellis;
   thocht he remissioun
   haif for prodissioun,
   schame and susspissioun
     ay with him dwellis.

And he evir odious as ane owle,
the falt sa filthy is and fowle;
   horrible to natour
   is ane tratour,
   as feind in fratour
     undir a cowle.

Quha is a tratour or ane theif,
upoun him selff turnis the mischeif;
   his frawdfull wylis
   him self begylis,
   as in the ilis
     is now a preiff.

The fell strong tratour, Donald Owyr,
mair falsett had nor udir fowyr
   round ylis and seyis;

in his suppleis,
on gallow treis
　　yitt dois he glowir.

Falsett no feit hes, nor deffence,
be power, practik, nor puscence;
　　thocht it fra licht
　　be smord with slicht,
　　god schawis the richt
　　　with soir vengence.

Off the fals fox dissimulatour,
kynd hes every theiff and tratour;
　　eftir respyt
　　to wirk dispyt
　　moir appetyt
　　　he hes of natour.

War the fox tane a thousand fawd,
and grace him gevin als oft for frawd,
　　war he on plane
　　all war in vane,
　　frome hennis agane
　　　micht non him hawd.

The murtherer ay murthour mais,
and evir quhill he be slane he slais;
　　wyvis thus makis mokkis
　　spynnand on rokkis;
　　'Ay rynnis the fox
　　　quhill he fute hais.'

WILLIAM DUNBAR

XI

Remonstrance to the King

Schir, ye have mony servitouris
and officiaris of dyvers curis;
kirkmen, courtmen, and craftismen fyne;
doctouris in jure, and medicyne;
divinouris, rethoris, and philosophouris,
astrologis, artistis, and oratouris;
men of armes, and vailyeand knychtis,
and mony uther gudlie wichtis;
musicianis, menstralis, and mirrie singaris;
chevalouris, cawandaris, and flingaris;
cunyouris, carvouris, and carpentaris,
beildaris of barkis and ballingaris;
masounis lyand upon the land,
and schipwrichtis hewand upone the strand;
glasing wrichtis, goldsmythis, and lapidaris,
pryntouris, payntouris, and potingaris;
and all of thair craft cunning,
and all at anis lawboring;
quhilk pleisand ar and honorable,
and to your hienes profitable,
and richt convenient for to be
with your hie regale majestie;
deserving of your grace most ding
bayth thank, rewarde, and cherissing.

And thocht that I, amang the laif,
unworthy be ane place to have,
or in thair nummer to be tald,
als lang in mynd my wark sall hald,
als haill in everie circumstance,
in forme, in mater, and substance,
but wering, or consumptioun,
roust, canker, or corruptioun,
as ony of thair werkis all,
suppois that my rewarde be small.

Bot ye sa gracious ar and meik,
that on your hienes followis eik
ane uthir sort, more miserabill,
thocht thai be nocht sa profitable:
fenyeouris, fleichouris, and flatteraris;
cryaris, craikaris, and clatteraris;
soukaris, groukaris, gledaris, gunnaris;
monsouris of France, gud clarat-cunnaris;
innopportoun askaris of Yrland kynd;
and meit revaris, lyk out of mynd;
scaffaris, and scamleris in the nuke,
and hall huntaris of draik and duik;
thrimlaris and thristaris, as thay war woid,
kokenis, and kennis na man of gude;
schulderaris, and schovaris, that hes no schame,
and to no cunning that can clame;
and can non uthir craft nor curis
bot to mak thrang, Schir, in your duris,
and rusche in quhair thay counsale heir,
and will at na man nurtir leyr:

in quintiscence, eik, ingynouris joly,
that far can multiplie in folie;
fantastik fulis, bayth fals and gredy,
off toung untrew, and hand evill deidie:
few dar, of all this last additioun,
cum in tolbuyth without remissioun.

And thocht this nobill cunning sort,
quhom of befoir I did report,
rewardit be, it war bot ressoun,
thairat suld no man mak enchessoun:
bot quhen the uther fulis nyce,
that feistit at Cokelbeis gryce,
ar all rewardit, and nocht I,
than on this fals world I cry, Fy!
my hart neir bristis than for teyne,
quhilk may nocht suffer nor sustene
so grit abusioun for to se,
daylie in court befoir myn e!

And yit more panence wald I have,
Had I rewarde amang the laif,
it wald me sumthing satisfie,
and les of my malancolie,
and gar me mony falt ouerse,
that now is brayd befoir myn e:
my mind so fer is set to flyt,
that of nocht ellis I can endyt;
for owther man my hart to breik,
or with my pen I man me wreik;
and sen the tane most nedis be,
in to malancolie to de,

[110]

or lat the vennim ische all out,
be war, anone, for it will spout,
gif that the tryackill cum nocht tyt
to swage the swalme of my dispyt!

XII

To the King

Schir, yit remembir as of befoir,
how that my youthe is done forloir
in your service, with pane and greiff;
gud conscience cryis reward thairfoir:
exces of thocht dois me mischeif.

Your clarkis ar servit all aboute,
and I do lyke ane rid halk schout,
to cum to lure that hes na leif,
quhair my plumis begynnis to mowt:
exces of thocht dois me mischeif.

Foryhet is ay the falcounis kynd,
bot ever the myttell is hard in mynd;
quhone the gled dois the peirtrikis preiff,
the gentill goishalk gois undynd:
exces of thocht dois me mischeif.

The pyat withe the pairtie cote
feynyeis to sing the nychtingale note,
bot scho can not the corchet cleiff,
for harsknes of hir carleche throte:
exces of thocht dois me mischeif.

Ay fairast feddiris hes farrest foulis;
suppois thay have no sang bot yowlis,
in sylver caiges thai sit at cheif;
kynd natyve nestis dois clek bot owlis:
exces of thocht dois me mischeif.

O gentill egill! how may this be?
quhilk of all foulis dois heast fle,
your leggis quhy do ye nocht releif,
and chirreis thame eftir thair degre?
exces of thocht dois me mischeif.

Quhone servit is all uther man,
gentill and sempill of everie clan,
kyne of Rauf Colyard and Johine the Reif,
no thing I gett nor conqueis can:
exces of thocht dois me mischeif.

Thocht I in courte be maid refuse,
and have few vertewis for to ruse,
yit am I cum of Adame and Eve,
and fane wald leif as utheris dois;
exces of thocht dois me mischeif.

Or I suld leif in sic mischance,
giff it to God war na grevance,
to be ane pykthank I wald preif,
for thay in warld wantis na plesance:
exces of thocht dois me mischeif.

In sum pairt of my selffe I pleinye,
quhone utheris dois flattir and feynye;
allace! I can bot ballattis breif,
sic barneheid leidis my brydill reynye:
exces of thocht dois me mischeif.

I grant my service is bot lycht;
thairfoir of mercye, and not of rycht,
I ask you, sir, no man to greiff,
sum medecyne gif that ye mycht:
exces of thocht dois me mischeif.

Nane can remeid my maledie
sa weill as ye, sir, veralie;
with ane benefice ye may preiff,
and gif I mend not haistalie,
exces of thocht lat me mischeif.

I wes in youthe, in nureice kne,
cald dandillie, bischop, dandillie,
and quhone that age now dois me greif,
a sempill vicar I can not be:
exces of thocht dois me mischeif.

Jok, that wes wont to keip the stirkis,
can now draw him ane cleik of kirkis,
with ane fals cairt in to his sleif,
worthe all my ballattis under the byrkis:
exces of thocht dois me mischeif.

Twa curis or thre hes uplandis Michell,
with dispensationis in ane knitchell,
thocht he fra nolt had new tane leif;
he playis with *totum* and I with *nychell*:
exces of thocht dois me mischeif.

How suld I leif and I not landit,
nor yit withe benefice am blandit?
I say not, sir, yow to repreiff,
bot doutles I go rycht neir hand it:
exces of thocht dois me mischeif.

As saule in to purgatorie,
leifand in pane with hoip of glorie,
so is my selffe ye may beleiff
in hoip, sir, of your adjutorie:
exces of thocht dois me mischeif.

WILLIAM DUNBAR

XIII

None may Assure in this Warld

Quhom to sall I compleine my wo,
and kythe my cairis ane or mo?
I knaw not, amang riche or pure,
quha is my freind, quha is my fo;
for in this warld may non assure.

Lord, how sall I my dayis dispone?
for lang service rewarde is none,
and schort my lyfe may heir indure,
and losit is my tyme bygone:
in to this warld may none assure.

Oft falsatt rydis with a rowtt,
quhone treuthe gois on his fute about,
and laik of spending dois him spure;
thus quhat to do I am in doutt:
in to this warld may none assure.

Nane heir bot rich men hes renown,
and pure men ar plukit doun,
and nane bot just men tholis injure;
swa wit is blyndit and ressoun;
for in this warld may none assure.

WILLIAM DUNBAR

Vertew the court hes done dispys;
ane rebald to renoun dois rys,
and carlis of nobillis hes the cure,
and bumbardis brukis benefys;
so in this warld may none assure.

All gentrice and nobilite
ar passit out of hie degre;
on fredome is led foirfalture;
in princis is thair no petie;
so in this warld may none assure.

Is non so armit in to plait
that can fra trouble him debait;
may no man lang in welthe indure,
for wo that lyis ever at the wait;
so in this warld may none assure.

Flattrie weiris ane furrit goun,
and falsate with the lordis dois roun,
and trewthe standis barrit at the dure,
exylit is honour of the toun;
so in this warld may none assure.

Fra everie mouthe fair wordis procedis;
in everie harte deceptioun bredis;
fra everie E gois lukis demure,
bot fra the handis gois few gud deidis;
sa in this warld may none assure.

Towngis now are maid of quhite quhale bone,
and hartis ar maid of hard flynt stone,
and eyn ar maid of blew asure,
and handis of adamant laithe to dispone;
so in this warld may none assure.

Yit hart and handis and body all
mon anser dethe, quhone he dois call
to compt befoir the juge future:
sen al ar deid or de sall,
quha sould in to this warld assure?

No thing bot deithe this schortlie cravis,
quhair fortoun ever, as fo, dissavis
withe freyndlie smylingis lyk ane hure,
quhais fals behechtis as wind hyne wavis;
so in this warld may none assure.

O! quho sall weild the wrang possessioun,
or gadderit gold with oppressioun,
quhone the angell blawis his bugill sture,
quhilk onrestorit helpis no confessioun?
into this warld may none assure.

Quhat help is thair in lordschips sevin,
quhone na hous is bot hell and hevin,
palice of lycht, or pit obscure,
quhair yowlis ar with horrible stevin?
in to this warld may none assure.

Vbi ardentes anime,
semper dicentes sunt Ve! Ve!
sall cry Allace! that women thame bure,
O quante sunt iste tenebre!
In to this warld may none assure.

Than quho sall wirk for warldis wrak,
quhone flude and fyre sall our it frak,
and frelie frustir feild and fure,
with tempest keyne and thundir crak?
in to this warld may none assure.

Lord! sen in tyme sa sone to cum
De terra surrecturus sum,
rewarde me with na erthlie cure,
bot me ressave *in regnum tuum.*
sen in this warld may non assure.

XIV

Lament for the Makaris

'Quhen He Wes Sek'

I that in heill wes and gladnes,
am trublit now with gret seiknes,
and feblit with infermite;
   Timor mortis conturbat me.

WILLIAM DUNBAR

Our plesance heir is all vane glory,
this fals warld is bot transitory,
the flesche is brukle, the Fend is sle;
    Timor mortis conturbat me.

The stait of man dois change and vary,
now sound, now seik, now blith, now sary,
now dansand mery, now like to dee;
    Timor mortis conturbat me.

No stait in erd heir standis sickir;
as with the wynd wavis the wickir,
wavis this warldis vanite;
    Timor mortis conturbat me.

On to the ded gois all Estatis,
Princis, Prelotis, and Potestatis,
baith riche and pur of al degre;
    Timor mortis conturbat me.

He takis the knychtis in to feild,
anarmit under helme and scheild;
victour he is at all mellie;
    Timor mortis conturbat me.

That strang unmercifull tyrand
takis, on the moderis breist sowkand,
the bab full of benignite;
    Timor mortis conturbat me.

He takis the campion in the stour,
the capitane closit in the tour,
the lady in bour full of bewte;
    Timor mortis conturbat me.

He sparis no lord for his piscence,
na clerk for his intelligence;
his awfull strak may no man fle;
    Timor mortis conturbat me.

Artmagicianis, and astrologgis,
rethoris, logicianis, and theologgis,
thame helpis no conclusionis sle;
    Timor mortis conturbat me.

In medicyne the most practicianis,
lechis, surrigianis, and phisicianis,
thame self fra ded may not supple;
    Timor mortis conturbat me.

I se that makaris amang the laif
playis heir ther pageant, syne gois to graif;
sparit is nocht ther faculte;
    Timor mortis conturbat me.

He hes done petuously devour,
the noble Chaucer, of makaris flour,
the Monk of Bery, and Gower, all thre;
    Timor mortis conturbat me.

The gude Syr Hew of Eglintoun,
and eik Heryot, and Wyntoun,
he hes tane out of this cuntre;
 Timor mortis conturbat me.

That scorpion fell hes done infek
Maister Johne Clerk, and James Afflek,
fra balat making and tragidie;
 Timor mortis conturbat me.

Holland and Barbour he hes berevit;
allace! that he nocht with us levit
Schir Mungo Lokert of the Le;
 Timor mortis conturbat me.

Clerk of Tranent eik he hes tane,
that maid the Anteris of Gawane;
Schir Gilbert Hay endit hes he;
 Timor mortis conturbat me.

He hes Blind Hary and Sandy Traill
slaine with his schour of mortall haill,
quhilk Patrik Johnestoun myght nocht fle;
 Timor mortis conturbat me.

He hes reft Merseir his endite,
that did in luf so lifly write,
so schort, so quyk, of sentence hie;
 Timor mortis conturbat me.

He hes tane Roull of Aberdene,
and gentill Roull of Corstorphin;
two bettir fallowis did no man se;
    Timor mortis conturbat me.

In Dumfermelyne he hes done roune
with Maister Robert Henrisoun;
Schir Johne the Ros enbrast hes he;
    Timor mortis conturbat me.

And he hes now tane, last of aw,
gud gentill Stobo and Quintyne Schaw,
of quham all wichtis hes pete:
    Timor mortis conturbat me.

Gud Maister Walter Kennedy
in poynt of dede lyis veraly,
gret reuth it wer that so suld be;
    Timor mortis conturbat me.

Sen he hes all my brether tane,
he will nocht lat me lif alane,
on forse I man his nyxt pray be;
    Timor mortis conturbat me.

Sen for the deid remeid is none,
best is that we for dede dispone,
eftir our deid that lif may we;
    Timor mortis conturbat me.

XV

The Dance of the Sevin Deidly Synnis

Off Februar the fyiftene nycht,
full lang befoir the dayis lycht,
I lay in till a trance;
and then I saw baith hevin and hell:
me thocht, amangis the feyndis fell,
Mahoun gart cry ane dance
off schrewis that wer nevir schrevin,
aganis the feist of Fasternis evin
to mak thair observance;
he bad gallandis ga graith a gyis,
and kast up gamountis in the skyis,
that last came out of France.

'Lat se,' quod he, 'Now quha begynnis;'
with that the fowll Sevin Deidly Synnis
begowth to leip at anis.
And first of all in dance wes Pryd,
with hair wyld bak and bonet on syd,
lyk to mak waistie wanis;
and round abowt him, as a quheill,
hang all in rumpillis to the heill
his kethat for the nanis:
mony prowd trumpour with him trippit,
throw skaldand fyre ay as thay skippit
thay gyrnd with hiddous granis.

[123]

Heilie harlottis on hawtane wyis
come in with mony sindrie gyis,
bot yit luche nevir Mahoun,
quhill preistis come in with bair schevin nekkis,
than all the feyndis lewche and maid gekkis,
blak Belly and Bawsy Brown.

Than Yre come in with sturt and stryfe;
his hand wes ay upoun his knyfe,
he brandeist lyk a beir:
Bostaris, braggaris, and barganeris,
eftir him passit in to pairis,
all bodin in feir of weir;
in jakkis, and stryppis and bonettis of steill,
thair leggis wer chenyeit to the heill,
frawart wes thair affeir:
sum upoun udir with brandis beft,
sum jaggit uthiris to the heft,
with knyvis that scherp cowd scheir.

Nixt in the dance followit Invy,
fild full of feid and fellony,
hid malyce and dispyte;
for pryvie hatrent that tratour trymlit.
him followit mony freik dissymlit,
with fenyeit wirdis quhyte;
and flattereris in to menis facis;
and bakbyttaris in secreit places,
to ley that had delyte;

and rownaris of fals lesingis;
allace! that courtis of noble kingis
of thame can nevir be quyte.

Nixt him in dans come Cuvatyce,
rute of all evill and grund of vyce,
that nevir cowd be content;
catyvis, wrechis, and ockeraris,
hud-pykis, hurdaris, and gadderaris,
all with that warlo went:
out of thair throttis thay schot on udder
hett moltin gold, me thocht a fudder,
as fyreflawcht maist fervent;
ay as thay tomit thame of schot,
feyndis fild thame new up to the thrott
with gold of allkin prent.

Syne Sweirnes, at the secound bidding,
come lyk a sow out of a midding,
full slepy wes his grunyie:
mony sweir bumbard belly huddroun,
mony slute daw and slepy duddroun,
him servit ay with sounyie;
he drew thame furth in till a chenyie,
and Belliall, with a brydill renyie,
evir lascht thame on the lunyie:
in dance thay war so slaw of feit,
thay gaif thame in the fyre a heit,
and maid thame quicker of counyie.

Than Lichery, that lathly cors,
come berand lyk a bagit hors,
and Ydilnes did him leid;
thair wes with him ane ugly sort,
and mony stynkand fowll tramort,
that had in syn bene deid.
Quhen thay wer entrit in the dance,
thay wer full strenge of countenance,
lyk turkas birnand reid;
all led thay uthir by the tersis,
suppois thay fyllt with thair ersis,
it mycht be na remeid.

Than the fowll monstir Glutteny,
off wame unsasiable and gredy,
to dance he did him dres:
him followit mony fowll drunckart,
with can and collep, cop and quart,
in surffet and exces;
full mony a waistles wallydrag,
with wamis unweildable, did furth wag,
in creische that did incres;
'Drynk!' ay thay cryit, with mony a gaip,
the feyndis gaif thame hait leid to laip,
thair lovery wes na les.

Na menstrallis playit to thame but dowt,
for glemen thair wer haldin owt,
be day and eik by nycht;

except a menstrall that slew a man,
swa till his heretage he wan,
and entirt be breif of richt.

Than cryd Mahoun for a Heleand padyane;
syne ran a feynd to feche Makfadyane,
far northwart in a nuke;
be he the correnoch had done schout,
Erschemen so gadderit him abowt,
in Hell grit rowme thay tuke.
Thae tarmegantis, with tag and tatter,
full lowd in Ersche begowth to clatter,
and rowp lyk revin and ruke:
the Devill sa devit wes with thair yell,
that in the depest pot of hell
he smorit thame with smuke.

XVI

Of the Nativitie of Christ

Rorate celi desuper!
Hevins distill your balmy schouris,
for now is rissin the bricht day ster,
fro the ros Mary, flour of flouris:
the cleir Sone, quhome no clud devouris,
surminting Phebus in the est,
is cumin of his hevinly touris;
et nobis Puer natus est.

Archangellis, angellis, and dompnationis,
tronis, potestatis, and marteiris seir,
and all ye hevinly operationis,
ster, planeit, firmament, and speir,
fyre, erd, air, and watter cleir,
to him gife loving, most and lest,
that come in to so meik maneir;
et nobis Puer natus est.

Synnaris be glaid, and pennance do,
and thank your Makar hairtfully;
for he that ye mycht nocht cum to,
to yow is cumin full humly,
your saulis with his blud to by,
and lous yow of the feindis arrest,
and only of his awin mercy;
pro nobis Puer natus est.

All clergy do to him inclyne,
and bow unto that barne benyng,
and do your observance devyne
to him that is of kingis King;
ensence his altar, reid and sing
in haly kirk, with mynd degest,
him honouring attour all thing,
qui nobis Puer natus est.

Celestiall fowlis in the are
sing with your nottis upoun hicht;
in firthis and in forrestis fair
be myrthfull now, at all your mycht,

for passit is your dully nycht,
Aurora hes the cluddis perst,
the son is rissin with glaidsum lycht,
et nobis Puer natus est.

Now spring up flouris fra the rute,
revert yow upwart naturaly,
in honour of the blissit frute
that rais up fro the rose Mary;
lay out your levis lustely,
fro deid tak lyfe now at the lest
in wirschip of that Prince wirthy,
qui nobis Puer natus est.

Syng hevin imperiall, most of hicht,
regions of air mak armony;
all fishe in flud and foull of flicht
be myrthfull and mak melody:
all *Gloria in excelsis* cry,
hevin, erd, se, man, bird, and best,
he that is crownit abone the sky
pro nobis Puer natus est.

WILLIAM DUNBAR

XVII

On the Resurrection of Christ

Done is a battell on the dragon blak,
our campioun Chryst confountet hes his force;
the yettis of hell ar brokin with a crak,
the signe triumphall rasit is of the croce,
the divillis trymmillis with hiddous voce,
the saulis ar borrowit and to the blis can go,
Chryst with his blud our ransonis dois indoce:
surrexit Dominus de sepulchro.

Dungin is the deidly dragon Lucifer,
the crewall serpent with the mortall stang;
the auld kene tegir with his teith on char,
quhilk in a wait hes lyne for us so lang,
thinking to grip us in his clows strang;
the mercifull Lord wald nocht that it wer so,
he maid him for to felye of that fang:
surrexit Dominus de sepulchro.

He for our saik that sufferit to be slane,
and lyk a lamb in sacrifice wes dicht,
is lyk a lyone rissin up agane,
and as gyane raxit him on hicht;
sprungin is Aurora radius and bricht,
on loft is gone the glorius Appollo,
the blisfull day depairtit fro the nycht:
surrexit Dominus de sepulchro.

[130]

WILLIAM DUNBAR

The grit victour agane is rissin on hicht,
that for our querrell to the deth wes woundit;
the sone that wox all paill now schynis bricht,
and dirknes clerit, our fayth is now refoundit;
the knell of mercy fra the hevin is soundit,
the Cristin ar deliverit of thair wo,
the Jowis and thair errour ar confoundit:
surrexit Dominus de sepulchro.

The fo is chasit, the battell is done ceis,
the presone brokin, the jevellouris fleit and flemit;
the weir is gon, confermit is the peis,
the fetteris lowsit and the dungeoun temit,
the ransoun maid, the presoneris redemit;
the feild is win, ourcumin is the fo,
dispulit of the tresur that he yemit:
surrexit Dominus de sepulchro.

ANONYMOUS

XVIII

To the City of London

London, thou art of townes A *per se*.
  Soveraign of cities, semeliest in sight,
of high renoun, riches, and royaltie;
  of lordis, barons, and many goodly knyght;
  of most delectable lusty ladies bright;
of famous prelatis in habitis clericall;
  of merchauntis full of substaunce and myght:
London, thou art the flour of Cities all.

Gladdith anon, thou lusty Troy Novaunt,
  citie that some tyme cleped was New Troy,
in all the erth, imperiall as thou stant,
  pryncesse of townes, of pleasure, and of joy,
  a richer restith under no Christen roy;
for manly power, with craftis naturall,
  fourmeth none fairer sith the flode of Noy:
London, thou art the flour of Cities all.

Gemme of all joy, jasper of jocunditie,
  most myghty carbuncle of vertue and valour;
strong Troy in vigour and in strenuytie;
  of royall cities rose and geraflour;

empresse of townes, exalt in honour;
in beawtie beryng the crone imperiall;
swete paradise precelling in pleasaure:
London, thow art the floure of Cities all.

Above all ryvers thy Ryver hath renowne,
whose beryall stremys, pleasaunt and preclare,
under thy lusty wallys renneth down,
where many a swanne doth swymme with wyngis fare;
where many a barge doth saile, and row with are,
where many a ship doth rest with toppe-royall.
O! towne of townes, patrone and not-compare:
London, thou art the floure of Cities all.

Upon thy lusty Brigge of pylers white
been merchauntis full royall to behold;
upon thy stretis goth many a semely knyght
in velvet gownes and cheynes of fyne gold.
by Julyus Cesar thy Tour founded of old
may be the hous of Mars victoryall,
whos artillary with tonge may not be told:
London, thou art the flour of Cities all.

Strong be thy wallis that about the standis;
wise be the people that within the dwellis;
fresh is thy ryver with his lusty strandis;
blith be thy chirches, wele sownyng be thy bellis;
riche be thy merchauntis in substaunce that excellis;
fair be thy wives, right lovesom, white and small;
clere be thy virgyns, lusty under kellis:
London, thow art the flour of Cities all.

[133]

Thy famous Maire, by pryncely governaunce,
  with swerd of justice the rulith prudently.
no Lord of Parys, Venyce, or Floraunce
  in dignytie or honoure goeth to hym nye.
  He is exampler, loode-ster, and guye;
Principall patrone and roose orygynalle,
  above all Maires as maister moost worthy:
London, thou art the flour of Cities all.

XIX

The Ballad of Kynd Kittok

My Gudame wes a gay wif, bot scho wes rycht gend,
  scho duelt furth fer in to France, apon Falkland Fell;
thay callit her Kynd Kittok, quhasa hir weill kend:
  scho wes like a caldrone cruke cler under kell;
thay threpit that scho deid of thrist, and maid a gud
    end.
  eftir hir dede, scho dredit nought in hevin for to duell.
and sa to hevin the hieway dreidles scho wend,
  yit scho wanderit and yeid by to ane elriche well.
    Scho met thar, as I wene,
      ane ask rydand on a snaill,
      and cryit, 'Ourtane fallow, haill!'
      and raid ane inche behind the taill,
    till it wes neir evin.

Sa scho had hap to be horsit to hir herbry
    att ane ailhous neir hevin, it nyghttit thaim thare;
scho deit of thrist in this warld, that gert hir be so dry,
    scho never eit, bot drank our mesur and mair.
Scho slepit quhill the morne at none, and rais airly;
    and to the yettis of hevin fast can the wif fair,
and by Sanct Petir, in at the yet, scho stall prevely:
    God lukit and saw hir lattin in and lewch his hert
        sair.
      And thar, yeris sevin
        scho levit a gud life,
        and wes our Ladyis hen wif:
        and held Sanct Petir at strif,
    ay quhill scho wes in hevin.

Sche lukit out on a day and thoght ryght lang
    to se the ailhous beside, in till ane evill hour;
and out of hevin the hie gait cought the wif gaing
    for to get hir ane fresche drink, the aill of hevin wes
        sour.
Scho come againe to hevinnis yet, quhen the bell rang,
    Saint Petir hat hir with a club, quhill a gret clour
rais in hir heid, becaus the wif yeid wrang.
    Than to the ailhous agane scho ran the pycharis to
        pour,
      and for to brew and baik.
      Frendis, I pray yow hertfully,
        gif ye be thristy or dry,
        drink with my Guddame, as ye ga by,
    anys for my saik.

XX

I yeid the gait wes nevir gane,
I fand the thing wes nevir fund;
I saw under ane tre bowane
a lows man lyand bund.
Ane dum man hard I full loud speik,
ane deid man hard I sing.
Ye may knaw be my talking eik
that this is no lesing.
And als ane blindman hard I reid
upoun a buke allane:
ane handles man I saw but dreid
in caichepule fast playane.
As I come by yone forrest flat,
I hard thame baik and brew.
Ane rattoun in a window satt
sa fair a seme coud schew;
and cumand by Loch Lomont huth
ane malwart tred a maw.
Gife ye trow nocht this sang be suth,
speir ye at thame that saw.
I saw ane gus wirry a fox
rycht far doun in yone slak;
I saw ane lavrock slay ane ox
richt he up in yone stak;
I saw ane weddir wirry ane wouf
heich up in a law;

the killing with hir mekle mouth
ane stoir horne cowd scho blaw;
the partane with hir mony feit
scho spred the muk on field;
in frost and snaw, wind and weit,
the lapstar deip furris teild.
I saw baith buck, da and ra
in merkat skarlet sell;
twa leisch of grew hundis I saw alswa
the pennyis doun cowd tell;
I saw ane wran ane watter waid;
hir clais wer kiltit hie;
upoun hir bak ane milstane braid
scho bure — this is no lie.
The air come hirpland to the toun
the preistis to leir to spell;
the hurchoun to the kirk made boun
to ring the commoun bell;
the mows grat that the cat wes deid
that all hir kin mycht rew.
Quhen all thir tailis are trew in deid,
all wemen will be trew.

ANONYMOUS

XXI

How the first Helandman of God was maid of ane hors turd in Argylle, as is said.

God and Sanct Petir was gangand be the way
heiche up in Ardgyle quhair thair gait lay.
Sanct Petir said to God in a sport word,
'Can ye nocht mak a Heilandman of this hors turd?'
God turnd owre the hors turd with his pykit staff
and up start a Helandman blak as ony draff.
Quod God to the Helandman, 'Quhair wilt thou
        now?'
I will doun in the Lawland, Lord, and thair steill a
        kow.'
'And thou steill a cow, cairle, thair thay will hang thee.'
'Quattrack, Lord, of that? for anis mon I die.'
God than he lewch and owre the dyk lap
and out of his scheith his gowlly outgatt.
Sanct Petir socht this gowly fast up and doun,
yit could not find it in all that braid rownn.
'Now,' quod God, 'heir a marvell! How can this be
that I sowld want my gowly and we heir bot thre!'
'Humff!' quod the Helandman and turnd him about
and at his plaid nuk the guly fell out.
'Fy!' quod Sanct Petir, 'thou will nevir do weill,
and thou bot new maid sa sone gais to steill.'
'Umff,' quod the Helandman and swere be yon kirk
'Sa lang as I may geir gett to steill, will I nevir wirk.'

ANONYMOUS

XXII

Ane anser to ane Inglis railar praising his awin genalogy.

Ye, Inglische hursone, sumtyme will avant
your progeny frome Brutus to haif tane,
and sumtyme frome ane Angell or ane sanct,
as *Angelus* and *Anglus* bayth war ane.

Angellis in erth yit hard I few or nane,
except the feyndis with Lucifer that fell.
Avant you, villane, of that lord allane,
tak thy progeny from Pluto, prince of Hell.

Becaus ye use in hoillis to hyd your sell,
Anglus is cum from *Angulus* in deid:
above all uderis Brutus bure the bell
quha slew his fader, howping to succeid.

Than chus you ane of thais, I rek not ader;
tak Beelzebub or Brutus to your fader.

GAVIN DOUGLAS

(c. 1475–1522)

XXIII

from *The Aeneid*

The batalis and the man I wil discrive
fra Troyis boundis first that fugitive
by fait to Ytail come and cost Lavyne,
our land and sey katchit with mekil pine
by fors of goddis abufe, from every steid,
of cruell Juno throu ald remembrit fede.
Gret pane in batail sufferit he alsso
or he his goddis brocht in Latio
and belt the cite fra quham, of nobill fame,
the Latyne pepill takyn heth thar name,
and eik the faderis, princis of Alba,
cam, and the wallaris of gret Rome alswa.

O thou my Muse, declare the causis quhy,
quhat majeste offendit schaw quham by,
or yit quharfor of goddis the drery queyn
sa feil dangeris, sik travell maid susteyn
a worthy man fulfillit of piete.
Is thare sik greif in hevynly myndis on hie?

Thare was ane ancyant cite hecht Cartage,
quham hynys of Tyre held intill heritage,

ennymy to Itail, standand fair and plane
the mouth of lang Tibir our forgane,
mighty of moblys, full of sculys seyr,
and maist expert in crafty fait of weir,
of quhilk a land Juno, as it is said,
as to hir special abuf al otheris maid.
Hir native land for it postponyt sche
callit Same — in Cartage sett hir see.
Thair war hir armys and here stude eik hir chair.
This goddess ettillit, gif werdis war nocht contrar,
this realme tobe superior and mastres
to all landis, bot certis netheles
the fatale sisteris revolve and schaw, scho kend,
of Trojane blude a pepill suld discend,
Valliant in were, to ryng wydquhar, and syne
Cartage suld bring ontill finale rewyne,
and clene distroy the realme of Lybia.
This dredand Juno, and forthirmor alswa
remembring on the ancyant mortell weir
that for the Grekis, to hir leif and deir,
at Troy lang time scho led befor that day —
for yit the causys of wreth war nocht away
nor cruell harm foryet ne out of mind,
ful deip engravyn in hir breist onkynd
the jugement of Paris, quhou that he
preferrit Venus, dispisyng hir bewte.
Als Trojane blude till hir was odyus,
for Jupiter engenderit Dardanus
(fra quham the Trojanis cam) in adultry,
and Ganymedes revist abuf the sky,

maid him his butler, quhilk was hir douchteris office —
Juno inflambit, musing on thir casis nice
the quhile our sey that salit the Trojanys
quhilkis had the ded eschapit and remanys
onslane of Grekis or of the fers Achill,
scho thame fordryvis and causys oft ga will
frawart Latium, quhilk now is Italy,
be fremmyt werd ful mony yeris tharby
catchit and blaw wydquhar all seys about.
Lo, quhou gret cure, quhat travell, pane and dowt
was to begin the worthy Romanys blude!

XXIV

from *King Hart*

I

King Hart, in to his cumlie castell strang
closit about with craft and meikill ure,
so semlie wes he set his folk amang
that he no dout had of misaventure,
so proudlie wes he polist, plane and pure,
with youthheid and his lustie levis grene,
so fair, so fresche, so liklie to endure,
and als so blyth as bird in symmer schene.

2

For wes he never yit with schouris schot,
nor yit ourrun with rouk or ony rayne;
in all his lusty lecam nocht ane spot,
na never had experience in to payne,
bot alway in to liking nocht to layne.
Onlie to Love and Verrie Gentilnes
he wes inclynit cleinlie to remane
and woun under the wing of Wantownnes —

3

Dame Plesance had ane pretty place besyd,
with fresche effeir and mony folk in feir,
the quhilk wes parald all about with pride,
so precious that it prysit wes but peir;
with bulwerkis braid and mony bitter beir;
syn wes ane brig, that hegeit wes and strang,
and all that couth attene the castell neir,
it maid thame for to mer amis and mang.

4

With touris grit and strang for to behald,
so craftlie with kirnellis kervin hie;
the fitschand faynis, floreist all of gold,
the grundin dairtis, scharp and bricht to se,
wald mak ane hart of flint to fald and fle
for terrour, gif thay wald the castell saill;
so kervin cleir that micht na crueltee
it for to win in all this warld avale —

[143]

5

Hapnit this wourthy quene upon ane day,
with hir fresche court, arrayit weill at richt,
hunting to ryd, hir to disport and play,
with mony ane lustie ladie, fair and bricht.
Hir baner schene, displayit and on hicht,
wes sene abone thair heidis, fair quhair thay ryd.
The grene ground wes illuminyt of the lycht.
Fresche Bewtie had the vangarde and wes gyde.

6

Ane legioun of thir lustie ladeis schene
folowit this quene, trewlie this is no nay.
Harde by this castell of this king so kene
this wourthy folk hes walit thame a way,
quhilk did the dayis watcheis to effray,
for seildin had thay sene sic folkis befoir,
so mirrelie thay muster and thay play,
withoutin outher brag or bost or schore.

7

The watcheis of the sicht wes sa effrayit,
thay ran and tauld the king of thair intent.
'Lat nocht this mater, schir, be lang delayit.
it war speidfull sum folk ye outwarde sent,
that culd rehers quhat thing yone peple ment,
syn you agane thairof to certifie.
For battell byd thay bauldlie on yon bent.
It war bot schame to feinye cowartlie.'

[144]

8

Youthheid upstart and cleikit on his cloik
was browdin all with lustie levis grene.
'Rise, fresche Delyte, lat nocht this mater soke.
We will go se quhat may this muster mene.
So weill we sall us it cope betwene
thair sall nothing pas away unspyit.
Syn sall we tell the king as we have sene,
and thair sall nothing trewlie be denyit.'

9

Youthheid furth past and raid on Innocence,
ane milk quhyt steid that ambilit as the wind,
and fresche Delyt raid on Benevolence,
throw-out the meid that wald nocht byd behind.
The beymes bricht almost had maid thame blind
that fra fresche Bewtie spred under the cloude.
To hir thai socht and sone thay culd hir find.
No saw thay nane never wes half sa proude.

10

The bernis both wes basit of the sicht
and out of messour marrit in thair mude,
as spreitles folkis on blonkis huffit on hicht,
both in ane studie starand still thay stude.
Fair Calling freschlie on hir wayis yuid
and both thair reynyeis cleikit in hir handis,
syn to hir Castell raid as scho war woude,
and festnit up thir folkis in Venus bandis.

11

Becaus thair come no bodwarde sone agane,
the king outsent Newgate and Wantownnes,
Grene Luif, Disport, Waistgude that nocht can lane,
and with thame freschlie feir, Fulehardynes.
He bad thame spy the cais, quhow that it wes,
and bring bodwart or him self outpast.
Thay said thay suld and sone thay can thame dres.
Full glaid thay glide as gromes unagaist.

12

On grund no greif quhill thay the grit ost se
wald thay nocht rest, the rinkis so thay ride.
Bot fra thay saw thair sute and thair sembly
it culd thame bre, and biggit thame to byd
Dreid of Disdane, on fute ran thame beside.
Said thame, 'Be war, sen Wisdome is away,
for and ye prik amang thir folk of pride,
apane ye salbe restit be the way.'

13

Fullhardynes full freschlie furth he flang
a fure leynth fer befoir his feiris five,
and Wantones, suppois he had the wrang,
him followit on als fast as he micht drive,
so thai wer lyk amang thame self to strive.
The fouresum baid and huvit on the grene.
Fresche Bewtie with ane wysk come belyve
and thame all reistit, war thay never so kene.

14

With that the foursum fain thay wald have fled
agane unto thair castell and thair king.
Thai gave ane schout and sone thay have thame sched
and bisselie thay kan thame bundin bring
agane unto thair quene and bandis thring
about thair handis and thair feit so fast
quhill that thay maid thame with thair tormenting
haly of thair lyvis half agast.

15

The watchis on the kingis wallis hes sene
the chassing of the folk and thair suppryse.
Upstart King Hart in propir ire and tein
and baldlie bad his folk all with him rise.
'I sall nocht sit,' he said, 'and se thame thryse
discomfit clein my men and put at under.
Na, we sall wrik us on ane uther wys,
set we be few to thame be fifty hounder.'

16

Than out thay raid all to ane randoun richt,
this courtlie king and all his cumlie ost,
his buirelie bainer brathit up on hicht,
and out thay blew with brag and mekle bost
that lady and hir lynnage suld be lost.
Thay cryit on hicht thair seinye wounder lowde.
Thus come thay keynlie, carpand one the cost.
Thay preik, thay prance, as princis that war woude.

17

Dame Plesance hes hir folk arrayit weill
fra that scho saw thay wald battell abide.
So Bewtie with hir vangarde gane to reill,
the greitest of thair ost scho can ourride.
Syn fresche Apport come on the tother syd.
So bisselie scho wes to battell boune
that all that ever scho micht ourtak that tide,
hors and men, with brount scho straik all doun.

18

Richt thair King Hairt he wes in handis tane
and puirlie wes he present to the quene,
and scho had fairlie with ane fedderit flayne
woundit the king, richt wonderfull to wene;
delyverit him Dame Bewtie unto sene
his wound to wesche in sobering of his sair,
bot alwayis as scho castis it to clene
his malady incressis mair and mair.

19

Woundit he wes and quhair yit he na wait
and mony of his folk hes tane the flicht.
He said, 'I yeild me now to your estait,
fair quene, sen to resist I have no micht.
Quhat will ye saye me nowe? For quhat plycht?
For that I wait I did you never offence,
and gif I have done ocht that is unrycht,
I offer me to your benevolence.'

20

Be this the battell wes neir vincust all.
The kingis men ar tane and mony slane.
Dame Plesance can on fresche Bewtie call,
bad hir command the folk to presoun plaine.
King Hairt sair woundit was, bot he wes fayne,
for weill he traistit that he suld recure.
The lady and hir ost went hame agane
and mony presoner tak in under hir cure —

21

This wourthy king in presoun thus culd ly
with all his folk, and culd thair nane outbrek.
Full oft thay kan upone Dame Pietie cry,
'Fair thing, cum doun a quhyle and with us speik.
Sum farar way ye micht your harmes wreik
than thus to murdour us that yoldin ar.
Wald ye us rew, quhair evir we micht ourreik,
We suld men be to you for evirmare.'

22

That answerd Danger and said, 'That wer grete doute,
a madin sweit amang sa mony men
to cum alane, bot folk war hir about —
that is ane craft my self culd never ken.'
With that scho ran unto hir lady kene;
kneland, 'Madame', scho said, 'keip Pietie fast.
Syth scho ask, no licence to hir len:
May scho win out, scho will play you a cast.'

23

Than Danger to the dure tuik gude keip
both nicht and day, that Pietie suld nocht pas,
quhill all fordoverit in defalt of sleip,
so bisselie fortravalit as scho was,
Fair Calling gaif hir drink it to ane glas.
Sone efter that to sleip scho went anone.
Pietie was war, that ilk prettie las,
and privelie out at the dure is gone.

24

The dure on char it stude; all wes on sleip,
and Pietie doun the stare full sone is past.
This Bissines hes sene and gave gud keip;
Dame Pietie hes he hint in armeis fast.
He callit on Lust and he come at the last.
His bandis gart he birst in peces smale.
Dame Pietie wes gritly feirit and agast.
Be that wes Comfort croppin in our the wall.

25

Sone come Delyte and he begouth to dance.
Grene Love upstart and can his spreitis ta.
'Full weill is me,' said Disport, 'of this chance,
for now I traist gret melody to ma.'
All in ane rout unto the dure thay ga,
and Pietie put thairin, first thame befoir.
Quhat was thair mair? 'Out, harro!', 'Taik and slay!'
The hous is wone withoutin brag or schoir.

26

The courtinis all of gold about the bed
weill stentit was, quhair fair Dame Plesance lay.
Than New Desyr, als gredie as ane glade,
come rinnand in, and maid ane grit deray.
The quene is walknit with ane felloun fray,
up glifnit, and beheld scho wes betraysit.
'Yeild you, madame,' on hicht can Schir Lust say.
A wourde scho culd nocht speik, scho wes so abaisit.

27

'Yeild you, madame,' Grene Lust culd say all sone,
'And fairlie sall we governe you and youris.
Our lord King Hartis will most now be done
that yit is law amang the nether bowris.
Our lang, madame, ye keipit thir hie towris.
Now thank we none bot Pietie, us suppleit.'
Dame Danger in to ane nuk scho lowris,
and quakand thair the quene scho lay for dreid.

28

Than Busteousnes come with brag and bost.
All that ganestude he straik deid in the flure.
Dame Plesance sad, 'Sall we thus gate be lost?
Bring up the king! Lat him in at the dure!
In his gentrice richt weill I dar assure.'
Thairfor sweit Confort cryit upone the king.
Than Bissines, that cunning creature.
To serve Dame Plesance sone thay can him bring.

29

So sweit ane smell as straik unto his hart
quhen that he saw Dame Plesance at his will!
'I yeild me, schir, and do me nocht to smart,'
the fair quene said upone this wys him till.
'I sauf youris, suppois it be no skill.
All that I have and all that mine may be
with all my hairt I offer heir you till,
and askis nocht bot ye be trew till me.'

30

Till that Love, Desire and Lust devysit,
thus fair Dame Plesance sweitlie can assent.
Than suddandlie Schir Hart him now disgysit,
on gat his amouris clok, or evir he stint.
Freschlie to feist thir amouris folk ar went.
Blythnes wes first brocht bodwarde to the hall.
Dame Chastite, that selie innocent,
for wo yeid wode and flaw out our the wall.

31

The lustie quene scho sat in the mid the deis.
Befoir hir stude the nobill worthy king.
Servit thay war of mony dyvers meis,
full sawris, sweit, and swyth thay culd thame bring.
Thus thay maid ane mirrie merschelling.
Bewtie and Love ane sait burde hes begoin.
In wirschip of that lustie feist so ding
Dame Plesance hes gart perce Dame Venus tun.

32

Quha is at eis quhen baith ar now in blis,
bot fresche King Hart that cleirlie is above
and wantis nocht in warld that he wald wis
and traistis nocht that evir he sall remove.
Sevin yeir and moir Schir Liking and Schir Love
off him thay have the cure and governance,
quhill at the last befell and swa behuif
ane changeing new that grevit Dame Plesance.

33

A morrowingtyde, quhen at the sone so schene
out raschit had his bemis frome the sky,
ane auld gudlie man befoir the yet was sene
apone ane steid that raid full easalie.
He rappit at the yet but courtaslie,
yit at the straik the grit dungeoun can din.
Syn at the last he schowtit fellonlie
and bad thame rys and said he wald cum in.

34

Sone Wantownnes come to the wall abone
and cryit our, 'Quhat folk ar ye thairout?'
'My name is Age,' said he agane full sone,
'May thou nocht heir langar how I culd schout?'
'Quhat war your will?' 'I will cum in but dout.'
'Now God forbid, in faith ye cum nocht heir.'
'Rin on thy way or thou sall beir ane rout,
and say the portar he is wonder sweir.'

[153]

35

Sone Wantownnes he went unto the king
and tald him all the cais quhow that it stude.
'That taill I traist be na leissing.
He wes to cum — that wist I, be the rude.
It dois me noy, be God, in bone and blude
that he suld cum sa sone. Quhat haist had he!'
The quene said, 'To hald him out war gude.'
'That wald I fayne war doin, and it micht be.' —

36

Be that wes Age enterit, and yit first
his branchis braid out bayr at mony bore.
Unwylkum was the cry quhen that thay wist,
for followand him thair come five hundreth score
off hairis that King Hart had none befoir,
and quhen that fair Dame Plesance had thame sene,
scho grevit and scho angerit weill more.
Hir face scho wryit about for propir teyne —

37

Richt as thir two ware talkand in feir,
ane hiddous ost thay saw come our the mure.
Decrepitus — his baner schane nocht cleir —
was at the hand with mony chiftanis sture.
A crudge bak that cairfull cative bure
and cruikit was his lathlie lymmis bayth;
but smirk or smile, bot rather for to smure;
But scoup or skift, his craft is all to scayth.

38

Within ane quhyle the castell all about
he seigit fast with mony sow and gyne,
and thay within gaif mony hiddowus schout,
for thay war wonder wa King Hart to tyne.
The grundin ganyeis and grit gunnis syne
thai schut without, within thai stonis cast.
King Hart sayis, 'Had the hous, for it is mine.
Gif it nocht our als lang as we may lest.'

39

Thus thay within had maid full grete defence,
Ay quhill thay micht the wallis thay have yemit,
quhill at the last thay wantit thame dispence,
evill purvayit folk for weir and sa weill stemit.
Thair tunnis and thair tubbis war all temit
and failyet was the flesche that wes thair fude,
and at the last Wisdome the best hes demit
King Hart suld yeild — thair wes na uther gude.

40

'And he be tynt, in parell put we all.
Thairfoir had wait and lat him nocht away.'
Be this thay harde the meikle foretour fall
quhilk maid thame in the dungeon to effray.
Than rais thair meikle dirdum and deray.
The barmekin birst, thai enterit in at large.
Heidwerk, Hoist and Parlasy maid grit pay
and Murmouris mo with mony speir and targe.

41

Quhen that thay saw na bute wes to defend,
Than in thay leit Decripitus full tyte.
He socht King Hart, for he full weill him kend,
and with ane swerde he can him smertlie smite
his bak in twa richt pertlie for dispyte,
and with the brand brak he both his schinnis.
He gaif ane cry, than Comfort fled out quyte,
and thus this bailfull bargane he begynnis.

42

Ressoun forfochtin wes and evill drest,
and Wisdome wes ay wanderand to the dure;
Conscience lay doun ane quhyle to rest
becaus he saw the king wourd waik and pure;
for so in dule he micht no langar dure.
'Go, send for Deid!' thus said he verament.
'Yit, for I will dispone of my thesaure,
Upon this wise mak I my Testament.

43

To fair Dame Plesance, ay quhen sche list ride,
my prowde palfray, Unsteidfastnes, I leif,
with Fikkilnes, hir sadill, set on side.
Thus aucht thair none of reassoun hir to reve.
To fresche Bewtie, becaus I culd hir heve,
Grein Appetite, hir servand for to be
to crak and cry alway quhill he hir deve,
that I command him straitlie, quhill he de.

44

Grein Lust, I leif to thee at my last ende
of Fantisie ane fostell fillit fow.
Youthheid, becaus that thou my barneheid kend,
to Wantounnes ay will I that thou bow.
To Gluttony that oft maid me our fow,
this meikle wambe, this rottin lever als
se that ye beir, and that command I you,
and smertlie hing thame both abone his hals.

45

To Rere Supper, be he amang that route,
ye me commend — he is ane fallow fine.
This rottin stomak that I beir aboute,
ye rug it out and reik it to him syne,
for he hes hinderit me of mony dine
and mony time the mes hes gart me sleip.
Myn wittis hes he waistit oft with wine,
and maid my stomak with hait lustis leip.

46

Deliverance hes oft times done me gude,
quhen I wes young and stede in tendir age.
He gart me ryn full rakles, be the rude,
at ball and boull — thairfoir greit weill that paige.
This brokyn schyn that swellis and will nocht swage
ye beir to him — he brak it at the ball —
and say to him that it salbe his wage.
This breissit arme ye beir to him at all.

47

To Chaistite, that selie innocent,
heir leif I now my Conscience for to scowre
off all the wickit roust that throw it went,
quhen scho for me the teiris doun culd powre,
that fair sweit thing, bening in everie bour,
that never wist of vice nor violence,
bot evirmore is mareit with Mesour,
and clene of Lustis curst experience.

48

To Fredome sall ye found and fairlie beir
this threidbair cloik, sumtime wes thik of wow,
and bid him for my saik that he it weir
quhen he hes spendit of that he hes now.
Ay, quhen his purs of penneis is nocht fow
quhair is his fredome than — full far to seik!
'A, yon is he wes quhylum till allow.
Quhat is he now? No fallow wourth ane leik.'

49

To Waistgude luk, and beir Neid that I lefe:
to Covatice syn gif this bleis of fire:
to Vant and Voky ye beir this rowm sleif:
bid thame thairin that thai tak thame thair hire:
to Bissines that nevir wes wont to tire
beir him this stule and bid him now sit doun,
for he hes left his maister in the mire
and wald nocht draw him out thocht he suld droun.

GAVIN DOUGLAS

50

Fulehardines, beir him this brokin brow
and bid him bawldlie bind it with ane clout,
for he hes gottin morsellis on the mow
and brocht his maister oft in meikle dout.
Syn sall ye eftir faire Dame Dangeir schout
and say, becaus scho had me ay at feid,
this brokin speir sum time wes stiff and stout
to hir I leif, bot se it want the heid.'

ANONYMOUS
(c. 1520)

XXV
Jok Upalland

Now is our king in tendir aige:
Christ conserf him in his eild
to do justice bath to man and pege
that garris our land ly lang onteild.
Thocht we do double pay thair wege,
pur commonis presently now ar peild,
thay ryd about in sic a rege
be firth, forrest and feild,
with bow, buklar and brand.
'Lo, quhair thay ryd in till our ry.
The divill mot sane yone company
I pray fro many hairt trewly.'
Thus said Jok Upalland.

He that wes wont to beir the barrowis
betwix the baikhous and the brewhous,
on twenty schilling now he tarrowis
to ryd the he gait by the plewis.

ANONYMOUS

'Bot wer I king bund haif gud fallowis,
in Norroway thay suld heir of newis:
I suld him tak and all his marrowis
and hing thame heich upoun yone hewis,
and tharto plichtis my hand.
Thir lordis and barronis grit
upoun ane gallowis suld I knit
that this doun treddit hes our quhit.'
This said Johine Uponland.

Wald the lordis the lawis that leidis
to husbandis do gud ressone and skill,
to chiftanis thair chiftanis be the heidis
and hing thame heich upoun ane hill.
Than micht husbandis lawbor thair steidis
and preistis mycht pattir and pray thair fill,
for husbandis suld nocht haif sic pleidis:
bayth scheip and nolt mycht ly full still,
and stakis still mycht stand.
'For sen thay red amang our durris
with splent on spald and rousty spurris,
thair grew no fruct in till our furris.'
Thus said Johine Uponland.

Tak a pure man a scheip or two
for hungir or for falt of fude
to five or sex bairnis or mo,
thay will him hing with raipis rud.

ANONYMOUS

Bot and he tak a flok or two,
a bow of ky and lat thame blud,
full falsly may he ryd or go.
'I wait nocht gif thir lawis be gud.
I schrew thame first thame fand.
Jesu, for thy holy passioun,
thou grant him grace that weiris the croun
to ding thir mony kingis doun.'
Thus said Johine Uponland.

SIR DAVID LINDSAY
(1486–1555)

XXVI

The Complaint and Publict Confessioun of the Kingis Auld Hound, callit Bagsche, directit to Bawte, the Kingis best belovit Dog, and his companyeonis. Maid at Command of King James the Fyft be Schir David Lindesay of the Mont, Knycht, Alias Lyoun King of Armes.

I

Allace, quhome to suld I complayne
in my extreme necessitie,
or quhameto sall I mak my maine?
In court na dog will do for me.
Beseikand sum for cherite
to beir my supplicatioun
to Scudlar, Luffra and Bawte
now, or the king pas of the toun.

2

I have followit the court so lang
quhill in gude faith I may no mair:
the countre knawis I may nocht gang:
I am so crukit, auld and sair
that I wait nocht quhare to repair:
for quhen I had authorite,
I thocht me so familiar
I never dred necessite.

[163]

3

I rew the race that Geordie Steill
brocht Bawte to the kingis presence:
I pray God lat him never do weill
sen syne I gat na audience,
for Bawte now gettis sic credence
that he lyis on the kingis nycht goun,
quhare I perforce for my offence
man in the clois ly like ane loun.

4

For I haif bene ay to this hour
ane wirrear of lamb and hog,
ane tyrrane and ane tulyeour,
ane murdreissar of mony ane dog.
Five foullis I chaist outthroch ane scrog,
quharefor thare motheris did me warie,
for thay war drownit all in ane bog —
speir at Jhone Gordoun of Pittarie,

5

quhilk in his hous did bring me up
and usit me to slay the deir:
sweit milk and meill he gart me sup:
that craft I leirnit sone perqueir:
all uther vertew ran arreir
quhen I began to bark and flyte,
for thare was nother monk nor frere
nor wife nor barne but I wald bite.

6

Quhen to the king the cace was knawin
of my unhappy hardines
and all the suth unto him schawin
how everilk dog I did oppres,
then gave his grace command expres
I suld be brocht to his presence.
Nochtwithstanding my wickitnes
in court I gat greit audience.

7

I shew my greit ingratitude
to the Capitane of Badyeno,
quhilk in his hous did find me fude
two yeir with uther houndis mo,
bot quhen I saw that it was so
that I grew hich into the court,
for his reward I wrocht him wo
and cruellie I did him hurt.

8

So thay that gave me to the king,
I was thare mortall enemie.
I tuke cure of na kind of thing
bot pleis the kingis majestie.
Bot quhen he knew my crueltie,
my falset and my plane oppressioun,
he gave command that I suld be
hangit without confessioun.

9

And yit becaus that I was auld,
his grace thocht petie for to hang me,
bot leit me wander quhare I wald.
Than set my fais for to fang me
and every bouchour dog doun dang me.
Quhen I trowit best to be a laird,
than in the court ilk wicht did wrang me,
and this I gat for my rewaird.

10

I had wirreit blak Makesoun,
wer nocht that rebaldis come and red;
bot he was flemit of the toun.
From time the king saw how I bled,
he gart me lay upon ane bed,
for with ane knife I was mischevit.
This Makesoun for feir he fled.
ane lang time or he was relevit.

11

And Patrik Striviling in Ergyle,
I bure him bakwart to the ground
and had him slane within ane quhyle,
war nocht the helping of ane hound.
Yit gat he mony bludie wound,
as yit his skin will schaw the markis.
Find me ane dog, quhare ever ye found,
hes maid sa mony bludie sarkis.

12

Gude brother Lanceman, Lyndesayis dog,
quhilk ay hes keipit thy laute
and never wirryit lamb nor hog,
pray Luffra, Scudlar and Baute
of me, Bagsche, to have pitie
and provide me ane portioun
in Dunfermeling, quhare I may dre
pennance for my extortioun.

13

Get be thare solistatioun
ane letter frome the kingis grace
that I may have collatioun
with fire and candil in the place.
Bot I will leif schort time, allace,
want I gude fresche flesche for my gammis:
betwix Aswednisday and paice
I man have leve to wirrie lambis.

14

Baute, considder well this bill
and reid this cedull that I send you,
and everilk point thareof fulfill
and now in time of mys amend you.
I pray you that ye nocht pretend you
to clym ouer hie nor do na wrang,
bot frome your fais with richt defend you
and tak exemple quhow I gang.

15

I was that na man durst cum neir me
nor put me furth of my lugeing;
na dog durst fra my dennar sker me
quhen I was tender with the king.
Now everilk tike dois me doun thring
the quhilk before be me war wrangit
and sweris I serve na uther thing
bot in ane halter to be hangit.

16

Thocht ye be hamelie with the king,
ye Luffra, Scudlar and Bawte,
be war that ye do nocht doun thring
your nychtbouris throw authorite,
and your exemple mak be me,
and beleif ye ar bot doggis.
Thocht ye stand in the hiest gre,
se ye bite nother lambs nor hoggis.

17

Thocht ye have now greit audience,
se that be you be nane opprest.
Ye wylbe punischit for your offence
from time the king be weill confest.
Thare is na dog that hes transgrest
throw cruelte, and he may fang him,
his majesty will tak no rest
till on ane gallous he gar hang him.

18

I was anis als far ben as ye ar
and had in court als greit credence,
and ay pretendit to be hiear,
bot quhen the kingis excellence
did knaw my falset and offence
and my pridefull presumptioun,
I gat none uther recompence
bot hoyit and houndit of the toun.

19

Wes never sa unkind ane corce
as quhen I had authorite;
of my freindis I tuke na force
the quhilkis afore had done for me.
This proverb, it is of verite
quhilk I hard red in till ane letter,
'Hiest in court, nixt the weddie',
without he gyde him all the better.

20

I tuke na mair compt of ane lord
nor I did of ane keiching knaif.
Thocht everilk day I maid discord,
I was set up abone the laif.
The gentill hound was to me slaif,
and with the kingis awin fingeris fed:
The sillie raichis wald I raif:
thus for my ill deidis wes I dred.

21

Tharfor, Bawte, luke best about
quhen thou art hiest with the king,
for than thou standis in greitest dout,
be thou nocht gude of governing.
Put na pure tike frome his steiding
nor yit na sillie ratchis raif.
He sittis abone that seis all thing
and of ane knicht can mak ane knaif.

22

Quhen I come steppand ben the flure,
all rachis greit roume to me red:
I of na creature tuke cure
bot lay upon the kingis bed,
with claith of gold thocht it wer spred:
for feir ilk freik wald stand on far:
with everilk dog I was so dred
thay trimblit quhen thay hard me nar.

23

Gude brother Bawte, beir thee evin,
thocht with thy prince thou be potent.
It cryis ane vengeance from the hevin
for till oppres an innocent.
In welth be than most vigilent
and do na wrang to dog nor beiche,
as I have, quhilk I do repent:
na Messane reif to mak thee riche

24

Nor for augmenting of thy boundis
Ask no reward, schir, at the king
quhilk may do hurt to uther houndis
expres aganis Goddis bidding.
Chais na pure tike from his midding
throw cast of court or kingis requeist,
and of thy self presume no thing
except thou art ane brutall beist.

25

Traist weill thare is none oppressour
nor boucheour dog, drawer of blude,
ane tyrrane nor ane transgressour
that sall now of the king get gude,
from time furth that his celsitude
dois cleirlie knaw the verite,
bot he is flemit for to conclude
or hangit hich upon ane tre.

26

Thocht ye be cuplit all to gidder
with silk and swoulis of silver fine,
ane dog may cum furth of Balquhidder
and gar you leid ane lawer tryne.
Than sal your plesour turne in pyne
quhen ane strange hounter blawis his horne
and all your treddingis gar you tyne;
than sall your laubour be forlorne.

27

I say no moir — gude freindis adew,
in dreid we never meit agane.
That ever I kend the court I rew:
was never wycht so will of wane.
Lat no dog now serve our soverane
without he be of gude conditioun.
Be he perverst, I tell you plane,
he hes nede of ane gude remissioun.

28

That I am on this way mischevit
the Erle of Hountlie I may warie:
he kend I had bene weill relevit
quhen to the court he gart me carie:
wald God I war now in Pittarie!
Because I have bene so ill dedie,
adew! — I dar no langar tarie
in dreid I waif in till ane wyddie.

XXVII

*Ane Suplication directit frome Schir David Lyndesay, Knicht,
to the Kingis Grace, in Contemptioun of Side Taillis.*

Schir, thocht your grace hes put gret ordour
baith in the Hieland and the Bordour,
yit mak I supplicatioun
till have sum reformatioun

of ane small falt, quhilk is nocht tressoun,
thocht it be contrarie to ressoun.
Because the matter bene so vile,
it may nocht have ane ornate style,
quharefor I pray your excellence
to heir me with greit pacience —
of stinkand weidis maculate
no man may mak ane rois chaiplat.
Soverane, I mene of thir side taillis
quhilk throw the dust and dubbis traillis
thre quarteris lang behind thare heillis
expres agane all commoun weillis.
Thocht bischoppis in thare pontificallis
have men for to beir up thare taillis
for dignite of thare office:
rychtso ane quene or ane emprice,
howbeit thay use sic gravite
conformand to thare majestie,
thocht thare rob royallis be upborne,
I think it is ane verray scorne
that every lady of the land
suld have hir taill so side trailland.
Howbeit thay bene of hie estait,
the quene thay suld nocht counterfait.
Quhare ever thay go, it may be sene
how kirk and calsay thay soup clene.
The imagis in to the kirk
may think of thare side taillis irk,
for quhen the wedder bene most fair,
the dust fleis hiest in the air

and all thair facis dois begarie.
Give thay culd speik, thay wald thame warie.
To se I think ane plesand sicht,
of Italie the ladyis bricht
in thare clething most triumphand
above all uther Christin land,
yit quhen thay travell throw the townis,
men seis thair feit beneth thare gownis
four inche abone thare proper heillis,
circulat about als round as quheillis,
quhare throw thair dois na poulder ryis
thare fair quhyte lymmis to suppryis.
Bot I think maist abusioun
to se men of religioun
gar beir thare taillis throw the streit
that folkis may behald thare feit.
I trow sanct Bernard nor sanct Blais
gart never man beir up thare clais:
Peter nor Paule nor sanct Androw
gart never beir up thair taillis, I trow.
Bot I lauch best to se ane nun
gar beir hir taill abone hir bun
for no thing ellis, as I suppois,
bot for to schaw hir lillie quhyte hois.
In all thare rewlis thay will nocht find
quha suld beir up thair taillis behind.
Bot I have maist in to despite
pure claggokis cled in roiploch quhyte
quhilk hes skant twa markis for thare feis,
will have twa ellis beneth thare kneis.

Kittok that clekkit wes yistrene,
the morne will counterfute the quene.
Ane mureland Meg that mylkis the yowis,
claggit with clay abone the howis,
in barn nor byir scho will nocht bide
without hir kyrtill taill be side.
In burrowis wantoun burges wyiffis
quha may have sydest taillis stryiffis,
weill bordourit with velvoit fine,
bot following thame, it is ane pine;
in somer quhen the streitis dryis,
thay rais the dust abone the skyis.
None may go neir thame at thare eis
without thay cover mouth and neis
frome the powder to keip thair ene.
Consider give thare cloiffis be clene
betwixt thare cleving and thare kneis.
Quha mycht behald thare sweitie theis
begairit all with dirt and dust,
that wer aneuch to stanche the lust
of ony mon that saw thame naikit.
I think sic giglottis ar bot glaikit
without profite to have sic pride,
harland thare claggit taillis so syde.
I wald thay borrowstounis barnis had breikkis
to keip sic mist fra Malkinnis cheikkis:
I dreid rouch Malkin de for drouth
quhen sic dry dust blawis in hir mouth.
I think maist pane, efter ane rane
to se thame towkit up agane.

[175]

Than, quhen thay step furth throw the streit,
thare faldingis flappis about thair feit,
thare laithlie lining furthwart flypit,
quhilk hes the muk and midding wypit.
Thay waist more claith within few yeiris
nor wald cleith fyftie score of freiris.
Quhen Marioun frome the midding gois,
frome hir morne turne scho strypis the nois,
and all the day, quhare ever scho go,
sic liquor scho likkith up also.
The turcumis of hir taill, I trow,
mycht be ane supper till ane sow.
I ken ane man quhilk swoir greit aithis
how he did lift ane kittokis claithis
and wald have done, I wait nocht quhat;
but sone remeid of lufe he gat:
he thocht na schame to mak it wittin
how hir side taill was all beschittin.
Of filth sic flewer straik till his hart
that he behovit for till depart.
(Quod scho) 'Sweit schir, me think ye rew.'
(Quod he) 'Your tail makis sic ane stew
that, be Sanct Bryde, I may nocht bide it.
Ye war nocht wise that wald nocht hide it.'
Of taillis I will no more indite
for dreid sum duddroun me despite.
Nocht withstanding I will conclude
that of side taillis can cum na gude
sider nor may thare hanclethis hide:
the remanent proceidis of pride,

and pride proceidis of the devill:
thus alway thay proceid of evill.

    Ane uther fault, schir, may be sene:
thay hide thare face all bot the ene.
Quhen gentill men biddis thame gude day,
without reverence thay slide away
that none may knaw, I you assure,
ane honest woman be ane hure.
Without thare naikit face I se
thay get no mo gude dayis of me.
Hails ane Frence lady quhen ye pleis,
scho will discover mouth and neis
and with ane humill countenance
with visage bair mak reverence.
Quhen our ladyis dois ride in rane,
suld no man have thame at disdane;
thocht thay be coverit, mouth and neis,
in that cace thay will nane displeis,
nor quhen thay go to quiet places,
I thame excuse to hide thare facis,
quhen thay wald mak collatioun
with ony lustie companyeoun,
thocht thay be hid than to the ene —
ye may consider quhat I mene.
Bot in the kirk and market placis
I think thay suld nocht hide thare facis.
Without thir faltis be sone amendit
my flyting, schir, sall never be endit.
Bot wald your grace my counsall tak,
ane proclamatioun ye suld mak

baith throw the land and borrowstounis
to schaw thare face and cut thare gownis —
nane suld fra that exemptit be
except the quenis majeste.
Because this mater is nocht fair,
of rethorik it man be bair.
Wemen will say this is no bourdis
to write sic vile and filthy wordis,
bot wald thay clenge thare filthy taillis
quhilk ouir the myris and middingis traillis,
than suld my wrytting clengit be:
none uther mendis thay get of me.
The suith suld nocht be haldin clos, —
Veritas non querit angulos.
I wait gude wemen that bene wise
this rurall ryme will nocht dispryse.
None will me blame, I you assure,
except ane wantoun glorious hure
quhais flyting I feir nocht ane fle.
Fair weill, ye get no more of me.

ALEXANDER SCOTT
(?1515–1583)

XXVIII

Ane New Yeir Gift to the Quene Mary quhen scho come first hame, 1562

Welcum, illustrat ladye and oure quene:
welcum, oure lyone with the floure delyce:
welcum, oure thrissill with the Lorane grene:
welcum, oure rubent rois upoun the ryce:
welcum, oure jem and joyfull genetryce:
welcum, oure beill of Albion to beir:
welcum, oure plesand princes maist of price:
God gif thee grace aganis this guid New Yeir!

This guid New Yeir we hoip with grace of God
salbe of peax, tranquillitie and rest:
this yeir sall rycht and ressone rewle the rod,
quhilk sa lang seasoun hes bene soir supprest:
this yeir ferme faith sall frelie be confest
and all erronius questionis put areir:
to lauboure that this life amang us lest
God gif thee grace aganis this guid New Yeir!

[179]

Heirfore addres thee dewlie to decoir
and rewle thy regne with hie magnificence:
begin at God to gar sett furth his gloir
and of his gospell gett experience:
caus his trew kirk be had in reverence:
so sall thy name and fame spred far and neir.
Now this thy dett to do with diligence
God gif thee grace aganis this guid New Yeir!

Found on the first four vertews cardinall,
on wisdome, justice, force and temperans:
applaud to prudent men, and principall
off virtewus life, thy wirschep till avance:
waye justice equale without discrepance:
strenth thy estait with steidfastnes to steir:
to temper time with trew continuance
God gife thee grace aganis this guid New Yeir.

Cast thy consate be counsale of the sage
and cleif to Christ hes kepit thee in cure,
attingent now to twentye yeir of aige,
preservand thee fra all misaventure.
Wald thou be servit and thy cuntre sure,
still on the commoun weill haif ee and eir:
preis ay to be protectrix of the pure,
so God sall gyde thy grace this gude New Yeir.

Gar stanche all stryiff and stabill thy estaitis
in constance, concord, cherite and lufe:
be bissie now to banisch all debatis
betwix kirkmen and temporall men dois mufe:

the pulling doun of policie reprufe
and lat perversit prelettis leif perqueir,
to do the best besekand God above
to gife thee grace aganis this guid New Yeir.

Att croce gar cry be oppin proclamatioun
undir grit panis that nothir he nor scho
off halye writ haif ony disputatioun
bot letterit men or lernit clerkis thairto:
for lymmer lawdis and litle lassis, lo,
will argunn bayth with bischop, preist and freir:
to dantoun this thou hes aneuch to do.
God gife thee grace aganis this gude New Yeir!

Bot wyte the wickit pastouris wald nocht mend:
thair vitious leving all the warld prescryvis.
Thay tuke na tent thair traik sould turne till end,
thay wer sa proud in thair prerogatyvis.
For wantonnes thay wald nocht wed na wyvis
nor yit leif chaste, bot chop and change thair cheir.
Now to reforme thair filthy licherous lyvis
God gife thee grace aganis this guid New Yeir!

Thay brocht thair bastardis with the skrufe thay skraip
to blande thair blude with barrownis be ambitioun.
Thay purchest pithles pardonis fra the Paip
to caus fond folis confide he hes fruitioun,
as God, to gif for synnis full remissioun
and saulis to saif frome suffering sorowis seir.
To sett aside sic sortis of superstitioun
God gife thee grace aganis this gude New Yeir!

Thay lost baith benefice and pentioun that mareit
and quha eit flesch on Frydayis was fyrefangit.
It maid na mis quhat madinnis thay miscareit
on fasting dayis, thay wer nocht brint nor hangit:
licence for luchrie fra thair lord belangit
to gif indulgence as the devill did leir.
To mend thate menye hes sa monye mangit
God gif thee grace aganis this guide New Yeir!

Thay lute thy liegis pray to stokkis and stanes
and paintit paiparis, wattis nocht quhat thay mene:
thay bad thame bek and bynge at deid mennis banes,
offer on kneis to kis, syne saif thair kin:
pilgrimes and palmaris past with thame betwene
Sanct Blais, Sanct Boit, blait bodeis ein to bleir.
Now to forbid this grit abuse hes bene
God gife thee grace aganis this guid New Yeir!

Thay tyrit God with tryfillis, tume trentalis,
and daisit him with daylie dargeis,
with owklie abitis to augment thair rentalis,
mantand mort mumlingis, mixt with monye leis.
Sic sanctitude was Sathanis sorcereis
Christis sillie scheip and sobir flok to smeir.
To ceis all sindrye sectis of hereseis
God gif thee grace aganis this guid New Yeir!

With mes nor matynes no wayis will I mell:
to juge thame justlie passis my ingyne.
Thay gyde nocht ill that governis weill thame sell
and lelalie on lawtie layis thair line.

ALEXANDER SCOTT

Dowtis to discus for doctouris ar devyne
cunning in clergie to declair thame cleir:
to ordour this, the office now is thine:
God gife thee grace aganis this gude New Yeir!

As beis takkis walx and honye of the floure,
so dois the faithfull of Goddis word tak frute:
as waspis ressavis of the same bot soure,
so reprobatis Christis buke dois rebute:
wordis without werkis availyeis nocht a cute.
To seis thy subjectis so in lufe and feir
that rycht and reasoun in thy realme may rute,
God gife thee grace aganis this gude New Yeir!

The epistollis and evangelis now ar prechit
but sophistrie or ceremoneis vaine:
thy pepill maist pairt trewlie now ar techit
to put away idolatrie prophaine,
bot in sum hartis is gravit new agane
ane image callit cuvatyce of geir.
Now to expell that idoll standis up plane
God gif thee grace aganis this gude New Yeir!

For sum ar sene at sermonis seme sa halye,
singand Sanct Davidis psalter on thair bukis,
and ar bot biblistis fairsing full thair bellie,
bakbytand nychtbouris, noyand thame in nuikis,
ruging and raifand up kirk rentis like ruikis,
as verrie waspis, aganis Goddis word makis weir.
Sic Christianis to kis with Chauceris kuikis
God gife thee grace aganis this gude New Yeir!

[183]

Dewtie and dettis ar drevin be dowbilnes:
auld folkis ar flemit fra yung faith professouris:
the grittest ay the grediar, I ges.
To plant quhair preistis and personis wer possessouris
teindis ar uptane be testament transgressouris:
credence is past off promeis, thocht thay sweir.
To punisch papistis and reproche oppressouris
God gif thee grace aganis this gude New Yeir!

Pure folk ar famist with thir fassionis new:
thay faill for falt that had befoir at fouth.
Leill labouraris lamentis and tennentis trew
that thay ar hurt and hareit north and south.
The heidismen hes *cor mundum* in thair mouth,
bot nevir with mind to gif the man his meir.
To quenche thir quent calamiteis so couth
God gife thee grace aganis this gude New Yeir!

Protestandis takis the freiris auld antetewme,
reddie ressavaris, bot to rander, nocht:
so lairdis upliftis mennis leising ouir thy reume
and ar rycht crabit quhen thay crave thame ocht:
be thay unpayit, thy pursevandis ar socht
to pund pure communis corne and cattel keir.
To wisy all thir wrangus workis ar wrocht
God gife thee grace aganis this gude New Yeir!

Paull biddis nocht deill with things idolatheit
nor quhair hypocrasie hes bene committit,
bot kirk mennis cursit substance semis sweit
till laud men with that leud burd lime ar byttit.

[184]

Giff thou persave sum senyeour it hes smittit,
solist thame softlie nocht to perseveir:
hurt nocht thair honour, thocht thy hienes witt it,
bot gratiouslie forgife thame this gude yeir.

Foirgifanis grant with glaidnes and gude will
gratis till all into your parliament,
syne stabill statutis steidfast to stand still
that barrone, clerk and burges be content.
Thy nobillis, erlis and lordis consequent
treit tendir to obtene thair hartis inteir
that thay may serve and be obedient
unto thy grace aganis this gude New Yeir.

Sen so thou sittis in saitt superlative
caus everye stait to thair vocatioun go:
scolastik men the scriptouris to descryve,
and majestratis to use the swerd also,
merchandis to trafique and travell to and fro,
mechanikis wirk husbandis to saw and scheir:
so salbe welth and weilfaire without wo
be grace of God aganis this guid New Yeir.

Latt all thy realme be now in reddines
with coistlie clething to decoir thy cors:
yung gentilmen for dansing thame addres
with courtlie ladyes cuplit in consors:
frak ferce gallandis for feild gemmis enfors,
enarmit knychtis at listis with scheild and speir
to fecht in barrowis bayth on fute and hors
agane thy grace gett ane guid man this yeir.

This yeir salbe imbassattis heir belyffe
for mariage frome princes, dukis and kingis:
this yeir within thy regioun sall arise
rowtis of the rankest that in Europ ringis:
this yeir bayth blythnes and abundance bringis,
naveis of schippis outthrocht the sea to sneir
with riches, raymentis and all royall thingis
agane thy grace get ane gude man this yeir.

Giffe sawis be suth to schaw thy celsitude
quhat berne sould bruke all Bretane be the sea,
the prophecie expreslie dois conclude
the Frensch wife of the Brucis blude suld be:
thou art be line fra him the nynte degree
and wes King Frances pairty, maik and peir:
so be discence the same sowld spring of thee
by grace of God agane this gude New Yeir.

Schortlie to concluid, on Christ cast thy confort
and chereis thame that thou hes under charge:
suppone maist sure he sall thee send support
and len thee lustie liberos at large.
Beleif that Lord may harbary so thy bairge
to mak braid Britane blyth as bird on breir
and thee extoll with his triumphand targe
Victoriuslie agane this guid New Yeir.

ALEXANDER SCOTT

Lenvoy

Prudent, maist gent, tak tent and prent the wordis
intill this bill with will thame still to face
quhilkis ar nocht skar to bar on far fra bawrdis
bot leale but feale may haell avaell thy grace.
Sen, lo, thou scho this to now do hes place,
resaif, swaif and haif ingraif it heir
this now for prow that thou sweit dow may brace
lang space with grace, solace and peace this yeir.

Lectori

Fresch fulgent flurist fragrant flour formois,
lantern to lufe, of ladeis lamp and lot,
cherie maist chaist, cheif charbucle and chois,
smaill sweit smaragde smelling but smit of smot,
noblest natour, nurice to nurtour, not
this dull indite, dulce double dasy deir,
send be thy sempill servand Sanderris Scott,
greiting grit God to grant thy grace gude yeir.

ANONYMOUS

XXIX

Hay trix, tryme go trix

1

The Paip, that pagane full of pride
he hes us blindit lang,
for quhair the blind the blind dois gyde,
na wonder thay ga wrang:
like prince and king he led the ring
of all iniquitie,
hay trix, tryme go trix, under the grene. etc. .

2

Bot his abhominatioun
the Lord hes brocht to licht;
his popische pride and thrinfald crowne
almaist hes loist thair micht;
his plak pardounis ar bot lardounis
of new found vanitie,
hay trix, tryme go trix. etc. .

3

His Cardinallis hes caus to murne,
his Bischoppis borne aback:
his Abbottis gat ane uncouth turne
quhen schavelingis went to sack.

With burges wyfis thay led thair lyfis
and sure better nor we,
hay trix, tryme go trix. etc. .

4

His Carmelites and Jacobinis,
his Dominiks had greit do,
his Cordeleiris and Augustinis,
Sanct Frances ordour to.
Thay sillie freiris, mony yeiris,
with babling blerit our e,
hay trix, tryme go trix. etc. .

5

The Sisteris gray, before this day,
did crune within thair cloister.
Thay feit ane freir, thair keyis to beir,
the feind ressave the foster,
syne in the mirk sa weill culd wirk
and kittill thame wantounlie,
hay trix, tryme go trix. etc. .

6

The blind Bischop, he culd nocht preiche
for playing with the lassis:
the syllie Freir behuffit to fleiche
for almous that he assis:

[189]

the Curat, his Creid, he culd nocht reid,
schame fall the cumpanie,
hay trix, tryme go trix. etc. .

7

The Bischop wald nocht wed ane wife,
the Abbote not persew ane,
thinkand it was ane lustie life
ilk day to have ane new ane,
in everie place ane uncouth face
his lust to satisfie,
hay trix, tryme go trix, etc. .

8

The Persoun wald nocht have ane hure
bot twa, and thay war bony:
the Vicar (thocht that he was pure)
behuiffit to have als mony:
the Parris Preist, that brutall beist,
he polit thame privelie,
hay trix, tryme go trix. etc. .

9

Of Scotlandwell the Freiris of Faill,
the lymmerie lang hes lestit:
the Monkis of Melros maid gude kaill
on Frydayis quhen thay fastit:

the sillie Nunnis caist up thair bunnis
and heisit thair hippis on hie,
hay trix, tryme go trix. etc. .

10

Of lait I saw thir lymmaris stand
like mad men at mischeif;
thinking to get the upper hand
thay luke efter releif,
bot all in vaine, go tell thame plaine,
that day will never be,
hay trix, tryme go trix. etc. .

11

O Jesus, gif thay thocht greit glie
to see Goddis word downe smorit,
the Congregatioun made to flie,
hypocresie restorit
with Messis sung and bellis rung
to thair idolatrie,
Marie God thank you, we sall gar brank you,
befoir that time trewlie.

NOTES

GENERAL

(1) *Spelling*

Four conventions may sometimes cause difficulty:

(i) The combination *a/e/o/y* + *i may* indicate a long vowel, not a diphthong. *sair* = sore : *cleir* = clear : *hoip* = hope : *pryis* = prize.

(ii) In the combination -*al* + consonant -*al* represents a sound which in Modern Scots is often represented by -*au*-. *walking*, e.g., = waking, *not* walking. The Mn. Scots form is *waukin*.

(iii) *quh*- corresponds to English *wh*-.

(iv) -*is* is usually pronounced -*s*, but for metrical reasons it may be treated as a separate unstressed syllable.

(2) *Consonants*

(i) *c/k* may correspond to English *ch*. *kirk* = church; *sic* = such.

(ii) -*ch*- may correspond to English -*gh*-. *bricht* = bright; *heich* = high; *lachand* = laughing; *strecht* = straight.

(3) *Vowels*

(i) -*a*- may correspond to English -*o*-. *lang* = long; *maist* = most.

(ii) -*i*- may correspond to English -*o*-, -*oo*-, -*ou*-, or -*u*-. *wid* = wood; *wirk* = work, *rin* = run; *ying* = young.

(4) *Accidence*

(i) In the noun -*is*-, -*ys* may be either a plural or a possessive ending.

(ii) In the present indicative active of the verb, where the subject is not the personal pronoun, or where the subject personal pronoun does not immediately precede the verb, the ending of the 1st, 2nd and 3rd person, singular and plural, is -*s*, -*is* or -*ys*. -*s*, -*is* or -*ys* is the invariable ending of the 2nd and 3rd singular.

(iii) -*and* is the ending of the present participle.

(iv) -*in*, -*yn* is the ending of the past participle in strong verbs.

(v) -*t*, -*it*, -*yt* are endings of the past participle in weak verbs.

NOTES

English linguistic and orthographic habits had already begun to affect Scots usage in the fifteenth century, and there are many apparent exceptions to all the observations listed above (which in any case are not intended to be exhaustive). For a more extended treatment of Scots in this period, see especially G. G. Smith, *Specimens of Middle Scots* (Edinburgh and London, 1902), and for individual words W. A. Craigie and A. J. Aitken, *A Dictionary of the Older Scottish Tongue* (Chicago and London, 1931-).

ABBREVIATIONS

D.O.S.T. = *Dictionary of the Older Scottish Tongue*
O.B.S.V. = *Oxford Book of Scottish Verse*
S.G.T.S. = Scottish Gaelic Text Society
S.T.S.   = Scottish Text Society

THE ANNUNCIATION

Text: Gray MS. (c. 1500), ff. 70a–71b. The style is unlike that of any other poem by Henryson. The New Testament source is *Luke* I, 26–38. The opening lines echo *Song of Solomon* VIII, 6–7. 'As writ (i.e. Holy Writ) can pruf' is a reference to this text. Stanza 4 refers to three Old Testament types of the Annunciation, the Burning Bush (*Exodus* III, 2), Aaron's Rod (*Numbers* XVII, 1–8), and Gideon's Fleece (*Judges* VI, 36–40). See Émile Mâle, *The Gothic Image* (Fontana Library edition, 1961), pp. 146–50.
6.8. *Termigant*: Satan.

THE TESTAMENT OF CRESSEID

Text: from the quarto edition of Henry Charteris (Edinburgh, 1593). The arguments advanced by Denton Fox (*Testament of Cresseid*, London, 1968) in favour of Thynne's 1532 edition, and Anderson's 1662 edition do not entirely convince, but in line 363 I have followed him in adopting Thynne's *beedes* for the *prayers* of Charteris.

NOTES

For a critical discussion of the poem see Introduction, pp. 18–21, J. MacQueen, *Robert Henryson* (Oxford, 1967) pp. 45–93, and the introduction to Fox's edition.

For the use of the testament form in narrative poetry, compare *King Hart* below, as also Lindsay's *The Testament and Complaynt of the Papyngo* and *The Testament of Squyer William Meldrum,* which concludes the *Historie of Squyer William Meldrum* (D. Hamer, ed., *The Works of* Sir David Lindsay, 4 vols., S.T.S., 1931–6, I, pp. 56–90, 146–96), the *Testament and Tragedie of Umquhile King Henrie Stewart of Gude Memorie* and the *Bischoppis Lyfe and Testament* (J. Cranstoun, ed., *Satirical Poems of the Reformation,* 2 vols., S.T.S., 1891–3, I, pp. 39–45, 193–200). Compare also Dunbar's *Testament of Mr Andro Kennedy,* and Villon's *Le Petit* and *Le Grand Testament.* See W. H. Rice, *The European Ancestry of Villon's Satirical Testaments* (New York, 1941).

THE TOD

Text: Bannatyne MS. (1568), ff. 310b–317b (ed. W. Tod Ritchie, 4 vols., S.T.S., 1928–34). A few readings have been adopted from the otherwise markedly inferior small octavo print of Thomas Bassandyne (Edinburgh, 1571). The poem has hitherto been printed, not as a unity, but as three distinct fables. The action however is continuous in a way which is not paralleled in any other group of Henryson's fables. In Bannatyne, the three are introduced by the words 'The Tod fallowis', and this title is echoed by the final line, 'and thus endis the talking of the tod.' Compare the reference to the poem's title in the final lines of *The Preiching of the Swallow* and *The Taill of the Wolf and the Wedder.* Bannatyne separates *The Tod* from Henryson's other fables; in his MS it is preceded by *The Houlate* and followed by *Orpheus and Eurydice.* It is difficult to avoid the conclusion that he intended the poem to be a single narrative and to stand apart from his other ventures in the fable/fabliau genre.

The two main sources for *The Tod* are Chaucer's *Nun's Priest's Tale* and Caxton's *The History of Reynard the Fox* (1481). See MacQueen, *Henryson,* pp. 208–21.

NOTES

For a critical discussion of the poem, see Introduction, pp. 21–26, and MacQueen, *Henryson*, pp. 135–53.

3.3. *had*: Bannatyne omits. 3.4. *lyttill*: Bassandyne. Bannatyne *joly*. 9.3. *and the*: Bassandyne. Bannatyne *that*. 11.5. *ane*: Bannatyne omits. 13.3. *Partlot*: Bannatyne *Coppok*. 15.3. *dayis*: Bassandyne. Bannatyne *day*. 15.4. *als*: Bassandyne. Bannatyne omits. 19.1. *spak*: Bassandyne. Bannatyne omits. 19.7. *breik*: Bassandyne. Bannatyne *beke*. 23.1. *thay*: Bassandyne. Bannatyne omits. 25.6. *out*: Bassandyne. Bannatyne omits. 30.6. *thair*: Bassandyne. Bannatyne omits. 31.3. *as*: Bassandyne. *of* Bannatyne. 31.4. *to taist it is, quha*: Bassandyne. Bannatyne, *quha tastis it and*. 33.6. *his*: Bassandyne. Bannatyne *him*. 38.1. *waryit ar*: Bassandyne. Bannatyne omits. 39.6. *the*: Bassandyne. Bannatyne omits. 43.7. *Than*: Bannatyne *bot*. *Wele*: Bannatyne *mele*. 45.6. *thig*: Bassandyne. Bannatyne *beg*. 49.2. *on*: Bassandyne. Bannatyne *in*. 54.5. *his*: Bassandyne. Bannatyne *a*. 56.7. *thame have hantit to*: Bannatyne *have hantit thame to*. 63.7. *devotioun*: Bannatyne *thy devotioun*. 64.5. *ane lawe*: Bannatyne *lawe*. Bassandyne *ane law*. 64.6. *ane*: Bassandyne. Bannatyne *and*. 66.5. *in*: Bannatyne *to*. 70.2. *thair*: Bannatyne *that*. 77.4. *standfray ar to*: Bassandyne. Bannatyne *standis aganis*. 80.1. *coit armour*: Bassandyne. Bannatyne *coit of armour*. 84.7. *fer*: Bassandyne. Bannatyne omits. 100.4. *thame*: Bannatyne omits. 101.6. *and pride*: Bannatyne *and all pride*. 102.6. *ring*: Bassandyne. Bannatyne *regne*. 104.7. *thame*: Bannatyne *him*.

THE TAILL OF RAUF COILYEAR

Text: from the quarto edition of Robert Lekpreuik (St. Andrews, 1572). I have made use of the facsimile, edited by Professor W. Beattie, and published by the National Library of Scotland (Edinburgh, 1966). See also *Scottish Alliterative Poems,* edited by F. J. Amours (S.T.S., 1897).

Sources and Date: The sources of the poem remain obscure, despite the stimulating discussion by M. P. McDiarmid in *Hary's Wallace* I (S.T.S., 1968), pp. cviii–cxxxii. McDiarmid suggests 1475 as a date for *Rauf*, and (less convincingly) that the author was the Blind Hary who wrote the *Wallace*. McDiarmid quotes 'the widespread story of how Philip, Duke of Burgundy, one rainy night in the winter of 1458 lost his way in the forest of Sogne and was sheltered in 'la Cabane d'un Charbonnier.'

NOTES

In the morning he was found by his attendants and grandly accompanied back to Brussels.' (*L'Histoire Des Ducs De Bourgogne Par Monsieur Fabert*, Cologne, 1689, I, pp. 152–4: *The Chronicles of Enguerrand de Monstrelet*, 2 (1877), p. 246.)

Rauf = Ralph; *Charlis*: Charlemagne.

1.4. *Sanct Thomas*: St Thomas' day, 21st December.

2.9. The *mirk montanis* stand in a forest (6.4), where a charcoal burner is able to ply his trade successfully. No such combination of mountain and forest is to be found in the vicinity of Paris; the poet clearly had in mind Ettrick Forest (generally called simply 'the Forest') and Edinburgh. Rauf is a typical Borderer of the late Middle Ages.

5.11. *Sanct July*: St Julian, patron of hospitality.

9.7. *but in the byre*. This phrase combines with *benwart thay yeid* (11.1) to show that Rauf's house was a 'but and ben' of two rooms, sharing a single entrance. Animals were kept 'but', in one apartment; humans lived 'ben' in the other. The *previe chalmer* (21.5) where the king sleeps is probably simply a curtained alcove, 'ben the hoose'. There is an ironic contrast between the actuality of the house and the language sometimes used by the poet to describe it. See John G. Dunbar, *The Historic Architecture of Scotland* (London, 1966), pp. 223–38.

10.2. Charles behaves as a king entertaining others in his own palace. Rauf resents his condescension.

12.2. The reader may suspect that Rauf's washing facilities were at best scanty.

The remainder of the story is as follows. Charles returns to Paris and on Christmas day sends Roland to watch for Rauf's arrival. Roland and Rauf quarrel, and agree to settle their dispute next day. Rauf arrives at the palace, where Charles knights him on condition that he wins his spurs. Next day Rauf sets out to meet Roland, but instead finds himself engaged with a strange knight on a camel — Magog, a Saracen, sent by the Khan of Tartary to threaten Charles. Roland witnesses Rauf's defeat of Magog, who is baptized as Sir Gawteir, and marries Dame Jane of Anjou. Sir Rauf is made Marshal of France, and founds 'a fair place' for travellers in the name of St. Julian at the spot where he met King Charles.

NOTES

JERUSALEM REJOS FOR JOY

Text: Bannatyne MS., ff. 27b–28a.

The refrain is taken from Isaiah LX, i: *Surge illuminare, Jerusalem; quia venit lumen tuum; et gloria Domini super te orta est.* In an abbreviated form, this text forms part of the Gradual in the Mass for Epiphany. The poem, with its emphasis on the Three Kings and the manifestation of Christ to the world, is clearly an Epiphany hymn.

WILLIAM DUNBAR

Text: For the poems by Dunbar and the two which follow, I have made use of the edition by W. Mackay Mackenzie (London, 1932; 2nd edition, revised by Bruce Dickins, 1960), and have consulted the selection edited by James Kinsley (Oxford, 1958).

ON HIS HEID-AKE

2.3. *sentence:* in medieval literary theory, the unifying idea or theme of a poem. 2.4. *heid behind:* a reference to the idea that the brain was divided into three cells, the front one assigned to fantasy, the middle one to reason, and the back one to memory. Memory is traditionally the mother of the Muses.

TO THE MERCHANTIS OF EDINBURGH

The poem is in fact addressed to the Town Council, the civil magistrates, of Edinburgh. In Scotland of the late medieval period, the Town Council and the Merchant Guild became virtually indistinguishable. See W. Croft Dickinson, *Scotland from the Earliest Times to 1603* (Edinburgh and London, 1961), p. 233.

3.1. *stinkand Scull:* unknown.

3.2. *your parroche kirk:* St. Giles.

3.3. *foirstairis:* outside stairs, giving access from the street to the upper storeys of houses. They were a common feature of Scottish burgh architecture. See Dunbar, *The Historic Architecture of Scotland,* pp. 170–81.

4.3. *Trone:* the burgh weighing machine, which also served as a pillory.

NOTES

Mn. Scots *Tron*. The commercial activity of a burgh centred on the Tron.

5.3. *Sanct Cloun*: an obscure Celtic saint. A church dedicated to such a saint, Dunbar implies, would be served by men of no musical education; their standards nevertheless would be higher than those of the common minstrels of Edinburgh.

6.3. *Stinkand Styll*: the Old-Kirk Style, an alley through the Luckenbooths, the crowded permanent shops or stalls to the east of St. Giles.

9.1. *Sessioun*: the supreme civil tribunal of Scotland.

EPETAPHE FOR DONALD OWRE

Dunbar may have hoped and expected that Donald Owre would be hanged, but in fact he outlived Dunbar and led another rising in 1545. John, the last MacDonald Lord of the Isles had been forfeited in 1493. His son Angus, had been murdered in or about 1490. Donald Owre was Angus's son, brought up by his maternal grandfather, the Earl of Argyll. During the 1490s he was in the service of James IV. In 1501 Torquil MacLeod of Lewis, Donald's uncle by marriage, began a rising against the King. Donald was imprisoned, but later released, only to find himself at the head of a major rebellion in the Western Isles, a rebellion which was not suppressed until 1506 when Donald was imprisoned in Stirling Castle. See especially R. L. Mackie, *King James IV of Scotland* (Edinburgh and London, 1958), chapters III and VII. With Dunbar's hostility to the MacDonalds, contrast the attitude of the Gaelic poets Giolla Coluim mac an Ollaimh and the Dean of Knoydart (W. J. Watson, *Scottish Verse from the Book of the Dean of Lismore*, S.G.T.S., 1937, poems X–XII).

Owre: Gaelic *odhar*, 'brown'.

With the last three stanzas, compare Henryson's *The Tod* above. Henryson quotes the final proverb in stanza 62.

REMONSTRANCE TO THE KING

See Introduction pp. 12–17.

66. *Cokelbeis gryce*: the reference is to the fifteenth century *Tale of*

NOTES

Colkelbie Sow, an anonymous comic narrative poem from the Bannatyne MS (ff. 357a–365a). Part 1 of the poem describes the feast given by a harlot to a very mixed company.

TO THE KING

In stanzas 2–6, the contrast is between neglected noble birds, hawks and nightingales, and the pampered lesser orders. The king, as eagle, climaxes the catalogue.

7.3. *Johine the Reif:* the hero of an English poem, the plot of which closely resembles *Rauf Coilyear* above.

10.3. Dunbar's reference to his poetry is of course ironic.

12.3. *ane benefice:* Dunbar probably never received a benefice. From 1500 onwards however he received a generous royal pension.

13.4. *a sempill vicar:* a vicar took the place of the *persoun* or rector of a parish. The rector continued to draw the stipend, for which he performed no parish duties, and from which he paid a small sum to the vicar.

15.4. *totum . . . nychell:* everything, nothing. 'A totum was a foursided disk made for a spinning toy, with a letter inscribed on each side: T (*totum*), A (*aufer*), D (*depone*), N (*nihil*). The player's fortune was set by the letter uppermost when the toy fell.' (J. Kinsley).

NONE MAY ASSURE IN THIS WARLD

Lindsay certainly had this poem in mind when he wrote his play *Ane Satyre of the Thrie Estaitis.* See especially stanza 8. Lindsay however lays more emphasis on Reformation than on the Last Judgement as the solution to the world's troubles. See the edition by J. Kinsley (London, 1954) or the modernized selection by M. P. McDiarmid (London, 1967).

15.1–2. 'Where the burning souls continue eternally to say Woe! woe!'
    4. 'O how great that darkness is.'

17.2. 'I am to rise from the earth.'
    4. 'into your kingdom'

NOTES

LAMENT FOR THE MAKARIS

The refrain ('the fear of death confounds me') is taken from the Office for the Dead, and the poem is the most extended expression of the pessimism which makes some appearance in so many of Dunbar's poems. ('Eftir our deid that lif may we' appears almost as an afterthought.) In form the poem is a Dance of Death in which all classes of society equally move towards the grave. Dunbar's procession is made up of the nobility and professional men, and lays a quite unusual emphasis on poets (But see Introduction pp. 12–14). The poem is not a lament, but the title seems likely to endure.

13.3. *Monk of Bery:* John Lydgate of Bury St. Edmunds.

14.1. *Sir Hew of Eglintoun:* ob. 1377. None of his poetry has survived.

2. *Heryot:* unknown.

Wyntoun: Andrew of Wyntoun (ob. 1422), author of the *Oryginale Chronykil of Scotland* (6 vols., S.T.S., 1903–14; see also O.B.S.V. pp. 19–22).

15.2. *Johne Clerk:* author of four poems in the Bannatyne MS (1568). See O.B.S.V. pp. 96–97.

James Afflek: unknown.

16.1. *Holland:* author of the *Buke of the Howlat* (c. 1450). See F. J. Amours (ed.), *Scottish Alliterative Poems* (S.T.S., 1897) and O.B.S.V. pp. 36–8.

Barbour: author of *The Bruce* (1376). See S.T.S. edition, 2 vols., 1894 and O.B.S.V., pp. 6–18.

3. *Schir Mungo Lokert:* ob. c. 1489. None of his poems have survived.

17.1. *Clerk of Tranent:* unknown.

3. *Schir Gilbert Hay:* (c. 1450). Translator from French. See S.T.S. edition of his prose works (2 vols., 1901, 1914).

18.1. *Blind Hary:* author of *The Wallace* (c. 1480). See S.T.S. edition (2 vols., 1968, 1969) and O.B.S.V., pp. 48–9.

Sandy Traill: unknown.

Patrik Johnestoun: possibly author of *The Thre Deid Pollis,* also attributed to Henryson. He belongs to the late 15th Century.

[200]

19.1. *Merseir:* author of three poems in the Bannatyne MS. See O.B.S.V., pp. 97–8.

20.1–2. *Roull of Aberdene* and *Corstorphin:* both are unknown, though one may be the author of *The Cursing of Schir Johine Rowlis,* preserved in the Bannatyne and Maitland MSS.

21.3. *Schir Johne the Ros:* friend and contemporary of Dunbar. See Walter Kennedy below.

22.2. *Stobo:* John Reid of Stobo (ob. c. 1505), possibly the author of the *Thrie Preistis of Peebles.* See S.T.S. edition (1920) and O.B.S.V., pp. 93–5.

Quintyne Schaw: ob. c. 1505. One of his poems has been preserved in the Maitland MS.

23.1. *Walter Kennedy:* author of four poems in the Bannatyne and Maitland MSS. See O.B.S.V., pp. 99–100. He was Dunbar's opponent in the flyting in which Dunbar was supported by Schir Johne the Ros.

THE DANCE OF THE SEVIN DEIDLY SYNNIS

The poem is a court entertainment, perhaps written to be performed on the evening of Shrove Tuesday (*Fasternis evin*), 1507. Shrove Tuesday that year fell on 16th February.

1.6. *Mahoun:* Mohammed, the Devil.

10. Notice again Dunbar's concern for poets.

11.5. *Erschemen:* Irishmen, i.e. Gaelic speakers.

OF THE NATIVITIE OF CHRIST

A Christmas hymn, built round the apparent paradox that Christ, the Sun of Righteousness, was born at midwinter. Much of the summer imagery of dew, flowers, light and growth gains force from the implied contrast with wintry actuality. The Latin texts, from the services for Christmas Eve and Christmas Day, are derived from Isaiah xlv. 8 and ix. 6.

[201]

NOTES

ON THE RESURRECTION OF CHRIST

A hymn for Easter Day. *Surrexit Dominus* 'the Lord has arisen', is the first versicle for Matins on Easter Day.

TO THE CITY OF LONDON

On the background and textual history of this poem, see Appendix C of W. Mackay Mackenzie's edition. It was written and performed in London in December 1501 by 'a Rhymer of Scotland', who was a member of the Scots party negotiating the marriage of James IV with Margaret Tudor. The Rhymer may or may not have been William Dunbar.

2.1. *Troy Novaunt:* New Troy. London was popularly supposed to have been founded by the Trojan Brutus, who gave it this name. The name is an etymological back formation from *Trinobantes,* the name of a Celtic tribe who inhabited the Colchester area.

2.7. *the flode of Noy:* i.e. since the beginning of the second age of the world. Obviously it was not possible for the foundation of any modern city to antedate Noah's flood.

4.7. *patrone:* pattern. So in 7.6.

THE BALLAD OF KYND KITTOK

1.2. *France — Falkland Fell:* an impossible comic juxtaposition. Falkland is in Fife.

I YEID THE GAIT

Text: Bannatyne MS., ff. 155b–156a.

HOW THE FIRST HELANDMAN

Text: Bannatyne MS., ff. 162b–163a.

NOTES

ANE ANSER TO ANE INGLIS RAILAR

Text: Bannatyne MS., ff. 163a–b. This is one of the earliest Scottish sonnets now extant.

4. *Angelus:* angel. *Anglus:* Englishman. Cf. the story of Pope Gregory, to be found in Bede's *Ecclesiastical History,* II. i.

10. *Angulus:* angle, nook, corner, lurking-place.

12. *quha slew his fader:* Geoffrey of Monmouth, *Historia Regum Britanniae* I.iii.

THE AENEID

Text: D.F.C. Coldwell (ed.), *Virgil's Aeneid Translated . . . by Gavin Douglas* (4 vols., S.T.S., 1957–64). This extract is Douglas's rendering of *Aeneid* I, 1–33. The greater length of Douglas's version is at least partly to be explained by the fact that he incorporated a commentary in his text. The version is the first great Renaissance translation to be produced in the British Isles, and was completed in 1513.

KING HART

Text: Priscilla J. Bawcutt, *The Shorter Poems of Gavin Douglas* (S.T.S., 1967). For a discussion of authorship, see pp. lxxii–lxxviii. The poem may well not be by Douglas. The narrative structure bears some resemblance to that of the first act of Lindsay's *Thrie Estaitis,* and may have some reference to the earlier years of James V's reign. King Hart and King Humanitie, Dame Plesance and Ladie Sensualitie bear an obvious resemblance to each other.

In the present text, I have omitted lines 17–96, 113–28, 257–336, 457–512 and 521–848.

42.8. Compare the note to Henryson's *Testament of Cresseid* above.

45.1. *Rere Supper:* late supper, after the main evening meal.

NOTES

JOK UPALLAND

Text: Bannatyne MS., ff. 93b–94a. The reference is to the period of James V's minority from Flodden (Sept. 1513) to the forfeiture of the Douglases in 1528. See the chapter on James V in Gordon Donaldson, *Scottish Kings* (London, 1967). 'Thir mony kingis' in the final stanza are probably the followers of Archibald Douglas, sixth Earl of Angus, who in 1514 had married the young widow of James IV.

Jok Upalland is an immediate ancestor of Lindsay's Johne the Commonweill in the *Dreme* and the *Thrie Estaitis*.

THE COMPLAINT ... OF BAGSCHE

Text: D. Hamer (ed.), *The Works of Sir David Lindsay* (4 vols., S.T.S., 1931–6), I, pp. 91–9. The poem was written between 1533 and 1536, and has doubtless a covert political meaning.

3.1. *Geordie Steill:* one of James V's courtiers who was also a minor poet. See J. MacQueen *Ballattis of Luve* (Edinburgh, 1969), pp. xxxiv–xxxv.

4.8. *Jhone Gordoun of Pittarie:* Pittarie is now Botary in Aberdeenshire, near Huntly, the seat of the Gordon Earls of Huntly.

7.2. *Badyeno:* Badenoch, Invernesshire. The Earls of Huntly ruled Badenoch.

10.1. *Makesoun:* James M'Kesoun, a lackey in the King's Wardrobe from 1531–42.

11.1. *Patrik Striviling:* Groom of the Chamber, 1525–40.

12.1. *Lyndesay:* probably the Earl of Lindsay.

13.7–8. Compare *The Tod* above, stanzas 47–8.

26.3. *Balquhidder:* in Perthshire. The reference is obscure.

28.8. *in dreid ... wyddie:* i.e. 'for fear I may be hanged.'

ANE SUPLICATION ... IN CONTEMPTIOUN OF SIDE TAILLIS

Text: Hamer, *op. cit.*, I pp. 118–22. The poem is later than 1537, the year in which James V, to whom it is addressed, married his first wife. See line 158.

NOTES

155 *land and borrowstounis:* the country areas and the burghs of regality and barony.

168 *Veritas non querit angulos:* Proverbial: 'Truth does not look for hiding places.'

ANE NEW YEIR GIFT TO THE QUENE MARY

Text: Bannatyne MS., ff. 90a–92a. In 1548, during her minority, Mary had been sent to France to ensure her safety from English intrusion. She returned on 19th August 1561, at the age of eighteen, to become the Catholic monarch of a country which since 1560 had been Protestant.

Alexander Scott may well have accompanied Mary to France in 1548. For his career as poet and professional musician see J. MacQueen, *Ballattis of Luve* (Edinburgh, 1969), pp. xxxv–xlvi. See also O.B.S.V., pp. 220–30.

The poem falls naturally into five sections, (i) personal advice to the Queen (ii) denunciation of pre-Reformation church practices (iii) denunciation of current social injustice (iv) anticipation of the Queen's marriage and the approaching unification of Britain (v) concluding flourish. For this and the following poem, see especially chapters 6–8 of G. Donaldson, *Scotland. James V to James VII* (Edinburgh and London, 1965), and the relevant studies in D. McRoberts (ed.), *Essays on the Scottish Reformation 1513–1625* (Glasgow, 1962).

1.2–3. Mary was queen of Scotland (the lion), and as wife of Francis II had been queen of France (the *fleur de lys*). The *Lorane grene* refers to Mary of Lorraine, James V's second wife and mother of Mary Queen of Scots.

8.1. *the wickit pastouris:* the pre-Reformation clergy.

16.7. '*Chaucer's Cuik* was an expression used to designate a thief or dishonourable person', J. Cranstoun, ed., *The Poems of Alexander Scott* (S.T.S., Edinburgh and London, 1896), p. 108.

18.5. *cor mundum:* 'pure heart'. The text is from Psalm L.12 (one of the Penitential psalms), *Cor mundum crea in me, Deus.*

25.3. *the prophecie:* attributed to Thomas the Rhymer.

27–28. Scott's contemporaries would have regarded the highly alliterative style of those two last stanzas as beautiful and effective.

HAY TRIX

Text: Ane Compendious Buik of Godlie Psalmes and Spirituall Sangis (Edinburgh, Henry Charteris, 1576). The expanded refrain should probably run *hay trix, tryme go trix, under the grene wode tree.*

4. This stanza refers to the different orders of Friars. Jacobins and Dominicans are the same. Cordeliers are the Franciscan Observantines, who wore a knotted cord round the waist.

9.1. *Scotlandwell . . . Faill.* Scotlandwell is in Kinross, Fail in Ayrshire. Both were houses of Trinitarian or Red Friars. See D. E. Easson, *Medieval Religious Houses. Scotland* (London, 1957), pp. 90–5.

11.3. *the Congregatioun:* the Congregation of Christ was an association of Protestant noblemen with their followers who in December 1557 pledged themselves to support Protestantism, and who eventually in 1560 obtained a more or less complete success.

GLOSSARY

A per se: the best, paragon
abaisit: abashed
abitis: offices for the dead (obits)
abject: outcast
abraid: flew
absens: absentees
aferit: was proper
affeir: appearance
air: (1) heir (2) hare (3) early
airschip: heirship
allkin: of all sort
allow: praise
als: also
alyte: a little
anarmit: armed
angrye: stern
antetewme: antiphone, response
apane: as a penalty
applidis: applied is (conforms herself)
apport: bearing, demeanour
are: oar
areir: behind
asis: assize
ask: newt
attonis: at once, together
attour: over, beyond
autentik: authoritative
avaell: profit, benefit

bacis: establishes

bagit hors: stallion
baid: waited
baill: woe, sorrow
bair: boar
bairge: barge
bait: halt for feeding horses
bakon: pig
bale: sorrow
ballaneis: balance
ballingaris: kind of boat
bankours: coverings
bannete: bonnet
bar: keep aloof
barganeris: wranglers
barmekin: outer fortification
barneheid: childishness
barret: trouble
barrowis: barriers
basare: executioner
basit: dismayed
baver } beaver
bawer }
bawrdis: jests
be: by; by the time that, when
befoir: before
beft: struck heavily
begarie: variegate
begouth   } began
begowthe }
behechtis: promises
behest: promise

[207]

GLOSSARY

behufe: use
beiche: bitch
beikit: warmed, basked
beild: covered over, decorated
beill: shelter, protection
beir: (1) bear (2) noise (3) buttress
beird: roared
beit: make better
bek: bow
beke: warn
belive: quickly
belly huddroun: glutton
belye: straightway
bene: are
bening: benign
bent: field, plain, grass, ground
berand: neighing
berk: bark
berne: child
bernis: knights, men
besy: busy, careful
bet: mended
betis: relieves
beuch: bough
biblistis: who make the Bible the
    sole rule of faith
biggit: begged
binge: cringe, bow
birkyn: birchen
bla: pale, discoloured
blaiknit: made pale
blait: simple
blandit: connected, associated
bleir: blind
bleis: torch
blenking: glancing

blin: stop, cease
blonkis: horses
blynnis: ceases
bodin: prepared
bodwarde: news
bogill: buffalo, wild ox
bolt: arrow
borrowit: ransomed, redeemed
bostaris: boasters
bot: (the soner bot) = unless
boull: game of bowls
boun: ready
bourd: joke
bowane: bending down
bown: ready, prompt
bowsumest: most buxom
bracis: encloses
brade: fly off
brag: bray, trumpet-blast
braid: sudden fright, start
braide: pull out
braiding: bursting into speech
braithlie: strongly
brand: sword
brandeist: swaggered
brank: to punish with the branks
    (iron bridle and gag)
brathit: lifted
brayd: broad
bre: alarm
breddit: started, sprang
breik: breech, hinder parts
breird (on): sprouting
brent: high, smooth
brist: burst
brok: badger

[208]

GLOSSARY

brount: force
bruke: possess
brukis: enjoys
brukkilness: frailty
brukle: brittle
brybours: vagabonds
brymly: loudly
brynt: inflamed
buird: table
buit: remedy
bukhud: hide-and-seek
bullar: bubble
bumbard: lazy, lazy fellow
bun: bottom
burde: table
burely: strong
buste: box
bustous: strong
but: without, outside
but bade: without bidding
bydand: waiting for
bynge: bend
byrd: should
byttit: bitten (metaphorical)

cachand: going
cachit: drove
caichepule: hand-tennis
cair: sorrow
cais: chance
caldrone cruke: chains for suspending pot over fire
calsay: causey, street
cant: brisk, smart
capill: horse

carie: escort
carit: made his way
carleche: rustic
carlingis: women of rude manners
carll: peasant
carpand: talking
carpin: speech
carping: chatter
carpit: spoke
cast: one's lot, fate
cative: wretched, miserable
cautelous: cunning
cavillatioun: trickery
cawandaris: [meaning obscure]
cedull: schedule
char, on: ajar
chaumer: chamber
chenyie: chain
cheif, at: in the place of honour
cheir: entertainment
cheis: choose
chere: face
cheverit: shivered, shook
chirreis: cherish
chois: choice
churle: man (in the moon)
claggokis: those clagged or muddied
claret-cunnaris: tasters, testers, connoisseurs of claret
clatteraris: babblers
claw: to scratch
cleiff: clef (in music)
cleik: haul or sweep (at cards)
cleikit on: pulled on
clek: hatch

GLOSSARY

clekkit: hatched, born

clour: lump or swelling caused by blow

cluke: claw

clyncheand: limping

coft: bought

coilis: charcoal

coilyear: charcoal-burner

coit: coat

collep: drinking-cup

compere: appear (in court)

con: squirrel

conding: worthy

conqueiss: acquire, gain

contumax: guilty of contempt of court

conyng } knowledge, ability,
connyng } learning

corchet: crotchet (music)

correnoch: coronach, war-cry, death-wail

cors: body

corse: person

cost: ground

coud: did

cought: did

countermaund: opposition

counyie: motion

couth: well-known

craig: (1) crag, hillock (2) neck

craikaris: boasters

crakraip: gallows-bird

cran: long

crawand: crowing

creillis: baskets

creische: grease

croppin: crept

crous: boldly, confidently

crudgebak: hunchback

cucheit: lay down

cunningar: more skilled

cunyng } rabbit(s)
cunningis }

cunyouris: coiners

curchis: kerchief, head-covering

cure: (1) care (2) cover

cute: jot

dantoun: overcome, suppress

dargeis: dirges

daw: dirty, untidy person

dawing: dawn

de: doe

debait: hesitation

decreit: purpose

dedie, ill: full of evil deeds

defence: (of grit defence = difficult of access)

defend: to uphold

degest: prepared

deid: death

deis: dais

deit: died

deray: noise, tumult, disturbance

deve: deafen

devidand: breaking into two halves

dicht: made ready

dine: dinner

ding: worthy, great

dirdum: uproar

[210]

GLOSSARY

disagysit: disguised
dispence: supplies
dispone: give away
divers: different
do: to cause (to do something)
doif: dull, slow
donk: moist
doolie: sad, doleful
dowbilness: duplicity
dowk: to duck, plunge
draff: brewer's grain
draif: drove
draw: withdraw
dreichlie: long and slowly
drery: cruel
dres: make ready
dress: (him dress = address himself, proceed)
drest: made ready
drevin: enacted
drift: driving snow
drope: village
drourye: sweetheart
drowpit (in dout): stood (in awe)
drowrie: love-token
drublie: wet
dubbis: puddles
duchepeiris: twelve peers of Charlemagne
duddroun: sloven, one clad in ragged clothes
dude: do it
dule: lament
dungeoun: keep (of castle)
dungin: overcome
durandlie: lastingly

duris, durris: doors
duschit: dashed
dyt, dyte: to write
dyte: writing, poem

effeir: appearance
effeirs: is proper
effray: take fright
elriche: frequented by fairies
enchessoun: occasion, objection
entent: thought, deed
entirt: entered
eth: easily
ettillit: intended
evintour (aventure): fortune, fate
excuse: have some excuse, reason

fachioun: falchion, large sword with curved blade
faind: missed
fair: ado, fuss
fairsing: stuffing
fald: lose heart
falset: falsehood
falt: want
faltum: fault them
fand: found
fang: catch
fant: faint
fayne: glad
faynis: metal vanes on tops of towers
fayr calling: courteous welcome
feale (but): without fail
fede: feud, enmity
feid: anger, ill-will

[211]

GLOSSARY

feir: (1) companion (2) strong (3) fear (4) demeanour
feir (in): together
feit: (1) feet (2) hired
feld: felt
fele: very great
fell: (1) hill, moor (2) dire, dreadful (3) befell, happened
felloun: deadly
felterit: matted
felye: fail
fens: formally open
fensum: offensive
fent: opening (of a garment)
fenyeit ⎱
feynit ⎰ deceitful
ferlyfull: awful
figurait: be likened in a figure
firthis: heaths
fitschand: moving
flan: storm
flane: arrow
flanis: arrows
flasche: sheaf
fleichouris: flatterers
flemit: banished, put to flight
flewer: odour
flingar: dancer
floreist: adorned
flowin: flown
flurist: adorned with blossom
flyrdome: humbug
foirfalt: to be forfeited
foirsaid: before-mentioned
fon: folly
force (of): of necessity

forcy: powerful
fordoverit: very drowsy
forfochtin: worn out with fighting
forgane: over against
forlane: forgotten, abandoned
forloir: entirely lost
forthy: therefore
foryeild: reward
foryhet: forgotten
fostell: flask
foster: child
foundis: goes
fouth: abundance
fra: from
frak: (1) bold (2) move quickly
frane: ask
fratour: refectory of a monastery
frawart: away from
freik: man
fremmyt: unfriendly
fronsit: wrinkled
frustir: destroy
fudder: great quantity
fude: food
fulfillit: gratified
full: fully, wholly
fumard: polecat
fure: (1) man (2) furrow (3) fared, proceeded
furrit: furred, trimmed
fusioun: abundance
fyber: beaver
fyrefangit: burned
fyre flawcht: lightning
fythow: fitchew

[212]

GLOSSARY

gair : gore (of dress)
gam : amusement
gammis : gums
gamountis : capers
ganecome : return
ganyeis : arrows
ganyie : arrow
garray : uproar
gate, gait : goat
gay : fair maid
gekkis : gestures of derision, gibes
gend : gentle
generabill : created
gent : beautiful
geraflour : gilly flower
get : begetting
giglot like : wantonly
giglottis : wanton girls
gird : struck
glade : kite
glaid : went (glide)
gle : entertainment
gled : red kite
gledaris : deceivers
glew : merriment, joy
glifnit : glanced
globert : glow-worm
glyid : go
govand : staring
gowlly : knife
graid : prepared
graith : get ready
grane : point
grant : promise
gree by gree : gradually
greissis : grass

greit : weeps
grete, grit : great
grewhundis : greyhounds
gromes : knights
grouf (on) : face downwards
groukaris : ? sharpers
groundin : ground sharp
gruncheing : grumbling
grund (on grund no grief) : they have no care in the world
grundin : sharpened
grunyie : snout
gryce : young pig
guckit : foolish
gudame : grandmother
guidis : goods, possessions
guye : guide
gyane : giant
gyis : (1) masquerade (2) fashion of garment
gyne : seige engine
gyse : dress
gyte : cloak

habirgeoun : sleeveless coat of armour
hace : hoarse
haifand : having
haldin owt : kept out
halk : hawk
hals : neck
hanclethis : ankles
hantit : practised
harbary, harberie : lodging, shelter
harland : dragging
harro : cry for help

GLOSSARY

hattrell : crown (of head)

haw : leaden, livid, bluish

hawtane : haughty, puffed up

haykit : went

hecht : promise, vow
: (I hecht — parenthetically — = I avow, I daresay)

heft : handle

hegeit : hedged, fenced about

heidis men : masters

heidwerk : headache

heilie : haughty

heill : health

heip (to bring to) : to bring about

heir : here

heisit : raised

hekill : hackle

hele : health, happiness

Heleand : Highland

herbry, herverye : shelter, lodging

hes : has

heve : vex

hewmound : helmet

hich : high

hicht (most of) : highest

hinder : last (this hinder yere = recently)

hine : hence

hint : seized

hir : her

hire : reward

hoir : hoarse, rough

hoise : hose

hoist : coughing

horlage : clock

how : hollow

hoyit : driven out by shouts of 'hoy'

huche : cliff, ravine

hud : hood, cowl

huddroun (belly) : glutton

hud-pykis : misers

huffit : poised

hurcheon, hurchoun : hedgehog

hurdaris : hoarders

hursoun : whoreson

huth = huch, heuch : steep side

huvit : halted

hy : haste

hyit : hurried

hyne : (1) hence (2) till

hynt : take

hynys : people

ilk : same

ilkane : each

indoce : indorse

infek (done) : rendered incapable

infild : undefiled

ingynour : contriver

inteir : wholly devoted

intentioun : charge, accusation

intermell : meddle

intill : into

irk : annoyance

ithand : continual

jakkis : jackets

joly : handsome

jonet : jennet (small Spanish horse)

josit : had, possessed

juperteis : tricks

GLOSSARY

katchit: driven
keir: drive off
kellis: headdresses
kend: recognised
kennattis: small hunting dogs
kepe, keip: guard
kest: cast about, sought
kethat: long coat
killing: cod-fish
kirnellis: battlement
kittill: tickle
knap doun: kill
knax: joking, quibbles
knitchell: small bundle
kokenis: rascals
kyith: make known
kythe: show

lair: to learn
laith: reluctant
lak: insult
lane, layne: deceive
lansand: bounding
lapstar: lobster
lardoun: ?
late: to search for
lathlie, lathly: loathsome
lattit: (let), prevented, hindered
laud: praise, fame, glory
laute: loyalty
law: hill, mound
lawer: lower
lawn: fine linen
lawtie: loyalty
lecam: body

leid: (1) lead (metal) (2) person, people
leif: leave
leip on: mount on horseback
leir: teach
leird: taught
leising, lesing: falsehood, lie
lelalie: loyally
leme: gleam
lemmane: sweetheart
lerit: taught
lerrion: ? dormouse
letis: ? thinks (Annunciation 1. 4)
leuch: laughed
leud: base
lewar: louver (opening in roof)
liberos: children
likand: pleasing, agreeable
lipper: leper
list: (1) hem, edging (2) are willing
loife: praise, flatter
lot: lotus
lour: skulk
lovery: bounty to servants, livery
low: flame
loweous: loose, immoral
lowris: crouches
Lowrye: fox (Lawrence)
lowt: stoop, bow down
luche: laughed
luchrie: lechery
luk: pay attention to
lunyie: loin
lurdane: villain
lusty: beautiful

GLOSSARY

lusumest: most lovable
lyand: building
lyart: grey, silvery grey
Lybell of repudie: bill of divorce
lymmar, lymmer: *adj.* vulgar,
      forward
      noun. rascal
lyre: skin, complexion, face

maik: mate
mair (but): without more ado
mak: compose poetry
malwart: mole
man: must
mang: go distracted
mangit: ruined
mantand: stammering
marrit: bewildered
martryk: marten
maw: gull
maynye: hurt
meis, mes: courses, meal
mekle: much
mellis: meddles
mendis: amends
mene: intend
mene (of): complain about
mene: means (by no mene =
  nohow)
menye: company, crew
menyie: to torture, pain
mer: bewildered
mer amis: come to utter confusion
merkand: resolving
mermissat: marmoset
Messane: lap-dog

miching: pilfering
middingis: middens
mild: gentle maid
ming: mingle
miscareit: seduced
mischevis: injures
mister: necessity
moblys: property
modewart: mole
modifie: assess, determine
moir: more
mony: many
more (without): at once, im-
  mediately
morsellis: blows
mort mumlingis: mumbled
  prayers for the dead
mow: mouth
mowaris: mockers
mowlit: mouldy
moyne: moon
mude: mind
muf: come
muirs: moors
musk: civet cat
mynis: means
mynyet: mingled
mys: wrong, sin
mysleving: misliving
mytell: kind of hawk?

nait: profit, occasion
nanis (for the): for the special
  occasion
neis: nose
nichtit: benighted

[216]

GLOSSARY

nois: nose
nolt: cattle
not: take note of
Noy: Noah
nycht: night

ochane: alas !
ockeraris: usurers
onwart: towards
opinioun: reputation
oratur: oratory, private chapel
ourhelit: laden, covered over
ourreik: travel
ourtane: overtaken
outwaill: outcast
owdir: either
owklie: weekly
owlk: week

padyane: pageant
paice: Easter
pairty: partner
Pais: Easter
palyoun: tent
pane: (1) part (2) cloth, dress
pansches: tripe
parlasy: paralysis
partan: crab
peild: pillaged, robbed
pench: paunch
perce: be broached
perqueir: (1) by heart (2) uprightly
pertlie: swiftly
perversit: corrupt
petie: pity
petpot: peathole

piking: stealing
plaine: directly
plait: coat of mail
plak: farthing
plane: cultivated land
plycht: crime
plye: condition
polit: fleeced
potingar: apothecary
preif: try, make trial, taste
preik: gallop
prent: impression
prys: praise
puirlie: ignominiously
pultry: poultry
pund: impound, distrain
pungitive: pricking, stinging
purchace: concubinage
pure: poor
pursevandis: heralds, messengers
pyat: magpie
pykit: pointed
pykthank: sycophant

quair: book
quhair: where
quhairin: wherein
quhen: when
quhilk: who, which
quhithrat: stoat
quik: living

raches, raichis: hunting dogs
raif: tear to pieces
raife: split open
raik: go, pass

GLOSSARY

rame : shout
rankest : noblest
rarit : called out
rattoun : rat
raw (on) : in a row, together
rawk : hoarse
rax : to have one's own way
rayth : swiftly
re : roe
rebaldis : persons of loose character
rebute : repel
red : (1) advice (2) divide,
    separate (3) remarked as,
    allowed
reif : n. robbery v. rob
reird : loud noise
rentis : income
repair : resort (maid his repair
    = went)
repudie : forsaking
respeit : exemption
ressoun : declaration
reume : realm
revand : ravenous
revar, rivere : robber
rew : the herb rue
reylock : pillage
rin, ryn : go one's own way
ringis : reigns
rinkis : men, warriors, knights
riyce, ryce : twigs
roiploch : coarse woollen cloth
rok (pl. rokkis) : distaff
ron : thicket, brushwood
rouch : hairy
rouk : mist

roune : whispering (done roun
    = whispered)
rousett : russet, homespun
roust : rust
rout : blow
rowm : wide
rownaris : whisperers
rowp : croak
rowtis : crowds
roy : king
Rude : the Cross
rufe : rest
rug : to tear, rend
ruik : rook
rumpillis : rough folds
ruse : praise
rute : take root
ryall : king
rycht : very
ryng : reign
ryvand : tearing
ryve : tear, destroy

sad : constant
saipheron : saffron
sait : spread
sane : say, bless
sare : sorely
sawris : savoury
scaffers : spongers
scamleris : intruders
scantlie : scarcely
schavelingis : ecclesiastics
schaw : wood
sched : separated
schene : bright, fair, beautiful

GLOSSARY

schent: destroyed

schill: (1) chill (2) shrill

scho: she

shoir, schore: menace, threat, threatening

schot: pelted

schrew: contrary person

schulderaris: that push with the shoulder

scoir: score

scoup: leap

serog: stunted brushwood

scrow: scroll

scull: school

se: see, look

seir: separate, various

seis: cease

selnye: battle-cry

sely: poor, innocent, unhappy

sembly: assembly

sen: since

ser: sir

set: although

seyr: many, several

sichand: sighing

sidlingis: on one side, sideways

sike: stream

sissokkis: low women

skar: shy

skift: skip

skill: reason, right
    : (that war but litill skill = that would be a foolish thing to do)

skraip: scrape together

skrufe: pelf, booty, riches

slak: small valley

sle: cunning, learned

slicht: cunning art

slute: slattern

smaragde: emerald

smit: stain

smord: smothered

smot: blot

smure: smother, destroy

sneir: spin

sobering: deliverance

soke: rest

soukaris: suckers, flatterers

sounyie: care

soup: sweep

soure: bitter

sow: a mining engine

sowpit: drowned

spald: limb

sparth: ?

speir: (1) ask (2) sphere

sperpellit: dispersed

spilt: spoiled, ruined

splent: arm: or leg-armour

stad: beset

stak: hill

standfray: opposed

stede: situated

steid: place

steird: upset

steiris: departs

stemit: esteemed

stentit: hung

stere: alarm, trouble

stevin: sound, voice

stint: stop, stopped

GLOSSARY

stoneist: alarmed

stound: pain

stowth: robbery

straik: stroke, blow

strakand: stroking

strypis: offends

stryppis: bands of steel, armour

stude: brood

studie: state of contemplation

sture: strongly

sturt: trouble

suith: truth

sumpart: shifting for oneself

suppleis: punishment

suppleit: aided

supplie: aid

supprype: defeat

sute: retinue

swaif: cherish

swak: throw

swalme: swelling

sweir: lazy

sweirnes: sloth

swelt: died, fainted

swentyouris: big, lazy fellows

swerde: sword

swoulis: swivels

swyith, swyth: straightway,
    swiftly

syde: long, hanging down

syis: often

sylit: covered

syne: then

syte: sorrow

ta: recover

taikning: token

tane: one or the other

targe: shield

tarye: delay

temit: emptied

tene, tein, teyne: anger

tere: use force to

thame: them

thane: then

thay dais: in these days, then

thig: beg

this: thus

tho: then

thocht, thouct: though

thoill: suffer

tholis: suffers, endures

thrawin: angry

threip: quarrel, maintain

thrimlaris: those that press forward
    in a crowd, pushers

thring: force

thring (doun): throw, kill

thristaris: thrusters

tide: time, season

tig: play, meddle

till: for

tod: fox

towkit: tucked

traik: trade, business

tramort: dead body

treddingis: trackings

trentalis: thirty masses for the
    dead

trip: flock

trumpir: deceiver

tryne: train, procession

GLOSSARY

tuitlyeour ⎱ brawler, bully addicted
tulyeour ⎰ to fighting
tun: cask
turcumis: filth
tyine: lose
tyke: dog, rascal
tyne: perish
tyt: (1) quickly (2) caught hold of

undynd: without dinner
uneis: hardly
unknawin: unknown
unrufe: unrest
uplandis: boorish
upricht: assuredly
ure: labour, toil

vant: vaunting
veiling: raising, doffing
verament: indeed
voky: vanity

wa: sorrowful
wag: shake
waif: swing
waillit: choice
waistles: without waist
wait: know
walcryif: watchful, unsleeping
wald: would
walit: chosen
wallydrag: slovenly woman
walterand: rolling
wambe, wame: belly, stomach
wan: (1) dull (2) gained, earned
wane: dwelling

wanhope: despair
wanis: dwellings
war: ready
warie: curse
warlo: warlock
watchis: watchman
watte: know
wayfe: watch, hunt about
wayndit: hesitated
weche: watch
weddie: gallows-rope
weddir: wether (sheep)
wederis: weather
wedow: widow
weir: (1) war (2) ward off
weir: (out of): without doubt
weit: wet
wellis: pools
welterit: overthrown, reversed
wem: blemish, stain
werd: fate, destiny
wicht: strong
wichtlie: strongly, fiercely
wickir: willow
widderit: faded
widdinek: gallows-bird
will: lost
will of wame: without hope
will of wane: wandering without
    a dwelling place
wirreit: worried, killed
wis: know
wisk: sudden, swift movement
wisy: enquire into
with: with, by
wod: mad

GLOSSARY

woik: stayed awake

woir (out): blew out or/kept out

wolk: week

wonder: wonderfully, very

woodwyss: wild man

worschip: honour

woun: live

wourd: became

wow: wool

wox: became

wrak: flotsam, rubbish

wrangus: wrongful

wreik, wrik: avenge

wryit: twisted

wude: wild

wydquhar: at large, everywhere

wyte: blame

yemit: guarded

yit: yet

yoldin: surrendered

INDEX OF FIRST LINES

[223]

INDEX OF FIRST LINES